Economists Are Morons

Table of Contents

Introduction

In my previous book, *Human Beings are Idiots*, I showed readers how our thought process fools people into believing that they are much smarter than they actually are. I showed readers that our ideas and our concept of reality are one in the same. The net effect of this being that no matter how ignorant, short-sighted or self-serving an individual's ideas about the world may be, those ideas will always appear to do an effective job at describing reality; fooling the individual into believing that their ideas represent the truth about the world we live in.

In that book I briefly discussed the effect this has had on our beliefs regarding science, religion and economics. In this book I am going to focus solely on how the thought process has fooled many people, including professional economists, into believing very strongly in some economic ideas that are clearly not true.

At the heart of the problem is an archaic educational system that is too heavily focused on merely handing out "facts"; such a system is so focused on "knowing" that it inevitably fails at helping people to "understand".

In our current educational system, we do not spend any time whatsoever helping people to understand the nature of the human thought process. Therefore, just as our ancestors were fooled by the thought process into thinking that their understanding of the universe was far more sophisticated than it really was, today we have been fooled into thinking that our understanding of our economy is far more sophisticated than it really is.

This problem is then exacerbated by the relatively recent explosion in the amount of data available in our world. The rapid expansion of the internet and proliferation in the number of television channels has made it much easier for us to transmit information to one another, but it has also made it **much easier to transmit misinformation**; and misinformation is usually much more appealing to the average end user.

Real information takes hard work to uncover and understand. It requires one to use logic and reasoning. It also requires one to look at the world from multiple perspectives. Unfortunately, our current educational system doesn't provide us with any of these skills.

Misinformation, on the other hand, is usually based on "common sense" ideas that are easy to understand and therefore appeal to a broad spectrum of individuals. The purpose of this book is to help you understand how these "common sense" ideas are hurting our economy.

Because our educational system is such a worthless piece of crap (from pre-school all the way through our PhD programs), we have great difficulty being able to distinguish between information and misinformation. We simply lack the skills needed to judge the quality of the material being presented to us.

To make matters worse, we have so much material to process on a daily basis that we tend to feel overwhelmed by it all. We don't feel that we have enough time to analyze all the data that we are currently being bombarded with; never mind trying to analyze the data from the last 40 years.

The net result is that we have naturally become much too short-sighted. We have become much too obsessed over the "crimes of the moment" and have completely lost sight of the economic big picture.

As just one example, consider the fact that there are millions of people who are currently convinced that our relatively recent financial crisis is the **cause** of our current economic malaise, when in reality it was merely a **symptom** of the fundamental problems facing our economy.

We have had such a hard time comprehending all the carnage from the recent financial crisis that we tend to completely ignore the fact that GDP growth rates have been declining for decades: (Figure 1)

Or the fact that wages have been trailing behind productivity for decades: (Figure 2)

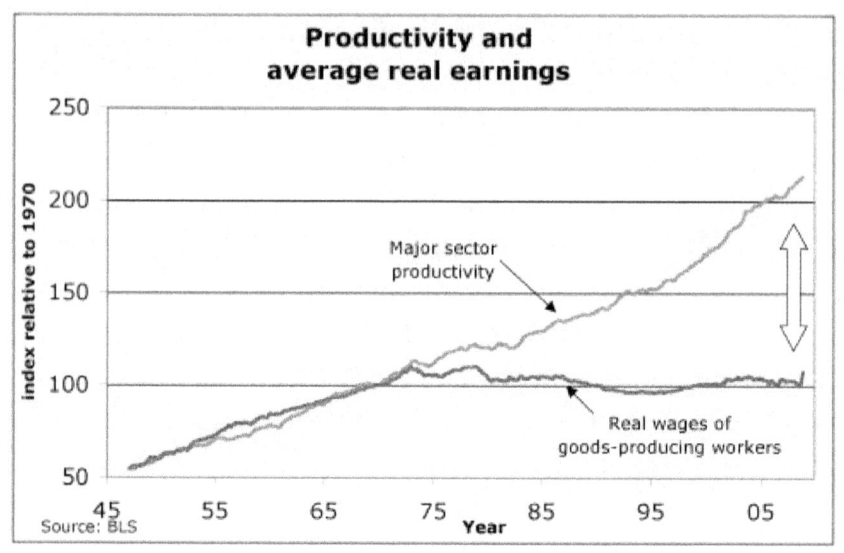

Or the fact that long-term unemployment has been rising for decades: (Figure 3)

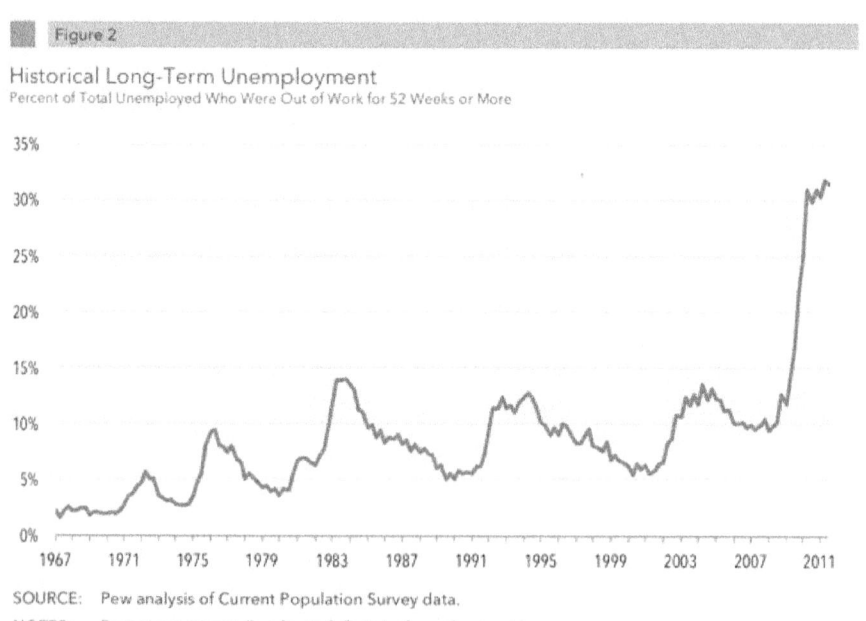

Or the fact that the business start-up rate has been declining for decades: (Figure 4)

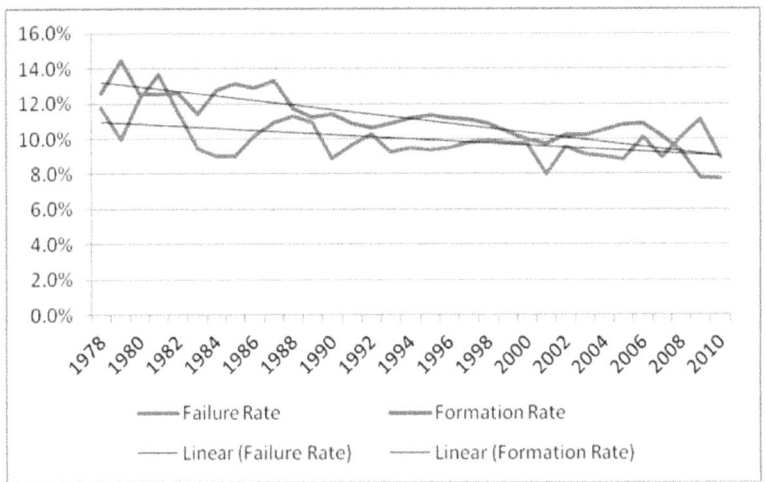

Source: Created from data from the Census Bureau's Business Dynamics Statistics

Or the fact that it has taken us longer to recover from each of the last four recessions: (Figure 5)

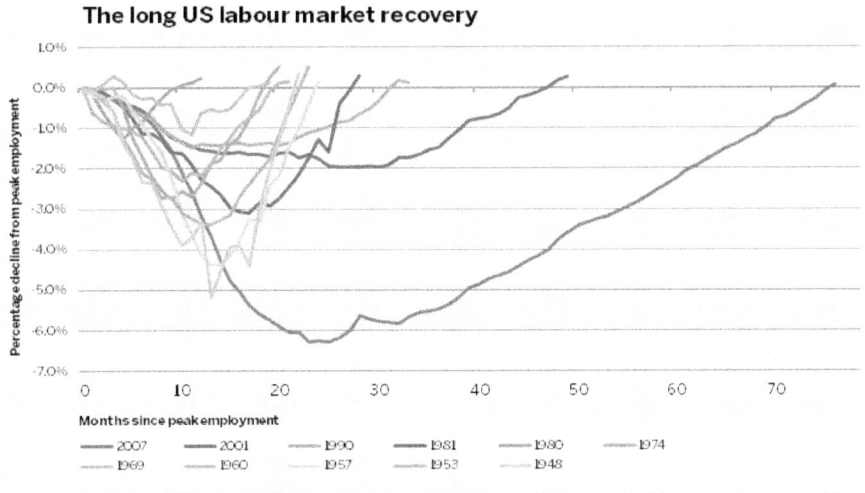

In short, we have failed to see that our economy has been in a long-term structural decline for decades. The kind of decline that is caused, not by the crimes of the moment, but by the weight of the fundamental beliefs (myths) that the economy is being forced to labor under.

By ignorantly focusing too heavily on the crimes of the moment in our economy instead of focusing on the beliefs that generate those crimes, we will naturally focus on situations like the Greece debt crisis or the collapse of Lehman Brothers and say "What did **they** do **wrong**?" without realizing that those situations are a natural byproduct of our general economic beliefs.

What is the hallmark of any competition? In any competition there are going to be winners and losers. After all, if somebody doesn't lose, then it is not a competition.

What is the hallmark of debt? Debt necessarily entails risk, and risk of course necessarily entails failure. After all, if you never fail at an activity, then you are not truly taking any risks.

So, we have a global economy that is based on competition and that is financed largely by debt, and *why exactly are you surprised when we have colossal failures?* If you are surprised by occurrences like Greece and Lehman Brothers, you might as well be surprised by the sun coming up in the morning or by grass being green.

Our current economic belief structure **guarantees** us a world that is going to be full of failures; both small and large. Being surprised at the arrival of these failures is completely illogical and irrational.

Over the course of the rest of this book, I will try and help you understand how our current belief structure is affecting our economy and is setting the stage for even more colossal failures in the future.

Here are a few quick technical notes before we get started. I tend to use the words "company", "business" and "corporation" almost interchangeably. Technically they are not all the exact same thing, but they are close enough for the purposes of this little book.

In addition, I tend to equate a company's stock price with its financial value. Again, technically they are not exactly the same, but they are close enough for the purposes of this little book.

I also tend to use the terms "income" and "revenue" interchangeably. Sometimes people will use the term "income" as a synonym for "profits" (i.e. Revenue minus Expenses). However, in this book "income" is used to describe monies that are *coming into* a business or person.

I suppose it is also worth mentioning that not all the myths in this book are supported by all economists. There are some who recognize the foolishness of the ideas being espoused by their intellectually addled brethren, but for whatever reason, they seem to be completely incapable of convincing the general public not to fall for such foolishness.

In addition, many of the economic *"experts"* that one often sees on TV or the internet are not actual economists at all. Instead they are more akin to a Teleconomist who, much like their Televangelist cousins, can attract followers not by the validity of their ideas, but by their charisma and their ability to play on the general public's profound level of ignorance of their chosen subject matter.

Myth 1: Wealth is Unlimited/Limited

Before we get started, it is important to mention that we are going to focus solely on the economic aspects of wealth. So, we will not count things like health, faith in God or happiness since we cannot place an economic value on them; even though one could easily argue that they are better measures of wealth in a more universal sense. Instead, we will focus our attention on items of material wealth such as stocks, gold, money, land, etc.

Now, in order for us to be able to understand the nature of this myth, we first need to understand that wealth, like all other human attributes, is paradoxical in nature. To help you understand this, let us take a quick look at a popular paradox known as the Bald Man Paradox.

If a man has no hair on his head, is he bald? Yes, he is. *If a man has one hair on his head, is he bald?* Yes, he is. *If a man has 10,000 hairs on his head, is he bald?* No, he is not. So where **exactly** is the line between **bald** and **not bald**?

Even though it seems clear that there are "bald" men and "not bald" men in the world, there is no specific line that separates the two, so it is impossible for us to create a universally true definition of "bald". No matter how hard we might try, we could never come up with an exact number of hairs that would truly separate bald men from not bald men.

To put this type of paradox in economic terms: *If a man has no pennies, is he poor?* Yes, he is. *If a man has one penny, is he* poor? Yes, he is. *If a man has 1,000,000,000,000,000 pennies, is he poor?* No, he is not. So where **exactly** is the line between **poor** and **not poor**?

Even though it seems clear that there are "poor" people and "not poor" (i.e. "rich") people in the world, there is no specific line that separates the two from each other, so it is impossible for us to create a universally true definition of "poor". No matter how hard we might try, we could never come up with an exact amount of wealth that would truly separate poor people from rich people.

This paradox comes to light whenever we discuss the issue of poverty here in the United States (US). According to government statistics, there are millions of people who are currently considered to be poor because they possess much less wealth than most other Americans. Not surprisingly, there are many people who feel that we clearly need to do something to help lift these poor people out of poverty.

On the other hand, there are also many people in this country who like to point out that even the poorest American is still way better off from an economic perspective than the majority of other individuals in the world. So there really is no need for us to go out of our way to improve their economic well-being.

So, which is true? Do we have millions of poor people in this country who need some type of economic assistance or should these people just be grateful that they are better off than most other people in the world?

What you need to recognize here is that neither of these beliefs is "true" in a universal sense. After all, saying that people should be happy simply because they are better off than some poor schmuck slogging through a rice field on the other side of the world makes no more sense than saying that people should be upset that they do not have as much wealth as a CEO of a large multinational corporation. Each of these viewpoints is entirely subjective, but due to the paradoxical nature of wealth, each of these viewpoints can **appear to be true**.

Because **any** set of ideas can **appear to be true**, human beings have an unerring tendency to believe in ideas that are ideally suited to their personal experience with the world. To see why I say this, consider the following.

Imagine an island nation where half the people live on the West side of the island and the other half live on the East side of the island. Currently the people on the West side are considered to be quite rich and the people on the East side are considered to be quite poor.

One day a magical fairy comes to the West side of the island. She is so struck with the hospitality of the "West-siders" that she decides to wave her magic wand and give them a little more wealth. The West-siders naturally express heartfelt gratitude towards the fairy. She is so moved by this that she decides to stop by and give them a little more wealth every day. This goes on for quite some time.

Not surprisingly, the poor people on the East side of the island begin to get a bit fed up with the situation. After years and years of watching the fairy continually give more wealth to the West-siders, the East-siders finally reach a breaking point. They decide that it is completely unfair for the fairy to only give wealth to half of the people on the island. So, they get together and develop a plan to beat the crap out of that fairy in order to stop her from giving any more wealth to the West-siders.

The West-siders hear about the plan and say "Hold on there! I don't see what you are getting so upset about. It is not like the fairy is doing anything to hurt you. She is not taking any wealth from you. She is just deciding to make us a little richer."

Meanwhile, the fairy sees the islanders arguing and starts to feel bad for the poor people on the East side. After thinking about the situation for a while, she decides that from now on she is going to give wealth only to the East-siders. So now when the fairy makes her daily visit, she waves her wand and only gives some wealth to the East-siders. After many years of this we find that the East-siders are now considered to be rich and the West-siders (who used to be rich) are now considered to be poor (because they now have less wealth than the East-siders).

In this situation, *do you think that the East-siders would still think that it was "unfair" for the fairy to only be giving wealth to half of the islanders? Do you think that the West-siders would still have absolutely no problem with what the fairy is doing*?

The lesson to be learned here is not that one side is "wrong" and the other is "right". The lesson to be learned here is that people in general do not act according to some "Great Truth" in the world. Instead, they act according to what they believe; and what they believe is almost always shaped by their own subjective experience with the world.

Because the views on economics of most Americans (including economists) are so subjective, these views generally tend to be quite naïve. The purpose of this book is to help you recognize the naïve nature of many of these beliefs and the impact these beliefs are having on our economy.

As we move along, it will become obvious that these naïve beliefs are causing the widening income gap in this country. This widening income gap has in turn led to the development of what are essentially two different "worlds" here in the US; the world of the "haves" and the world of the "have-nots".

Not surprisingly, the development of these two different "worlds" has naturally led to the development of two very different sets of ideas about the economy in general. Just as each group on the island in our earlier example developed very different ideas about whether or not it was "fair" for the fairy to only give wealth to half of the islanders, the "haves" and the "have-nots" here in the US have naturally developed very different ideas about our economy because they have had very different experiences with the economy.

The net result being that each political party in this country has essentially been forced to create policies that appeal to very different subsets of the overall population. These different sets of policies have naturally become increasingly dissimilar from one another as the wealth gap continues to increase, thus creating an increasingly contentious level of debate over what we should do about our economic situation.

In short, the Democrats have generally proposed that the wealth gap is being driven by our economic **system**. They propose that the rules and regulations that govern economic activity have all been structured to favor the rich. Therefore, they tend to focus on changing the rules of the game in order to reduce inequality.

On the other hand, the Republicans have generally proposed that the wealth gap is being driven by a lack of economic **growth**. They generally seek to try and grow our economy by reducing the amount of rules and regulations that govern our system. They believe that this will help improve the economic well-being of the working class and thus alleviate their economic angst.

Unfortunately for all of us, we will see throughout the rest of this book that neither of these views is True; neither party is truly addressing the real drivers of wealth inequality in this country. Thus neither party is going to be able to effectively remedy the situation. Instead, we will be locked in an unending series of pointless debates and political flip flops for the next several decades.

In order to overcome our current situation, we need to recognize that it is the limited nature of our beliefs that is leading to the widening wealth gap in the first place. A good place to start can be found in understanding how the wealth gap affects our views on the nature of wealth.

Because it is seemingly impossible for them to garner any wealth for themselves, the have-nots will often describe wealth as being like a big pie, where there is only a certain amount available to everybody. In their minds, if I keep a bunch of wealth for myself, I am preventing other people from being able to have any wealth. Therefore, they tend to advocate policies which attempt to force the haves to share their wealth.

On the other hand, the haves tend to describe wealth as being like an infinite ocean where there is no limit to the amount of wealth available to us all. In their minds, if I keep a bunch of wealth for myself, I am not preventing you from having wealth because you can simply go out and create some for yourself. Therefore, they tend to support policies that allow people to freely pursue their own wealth.

So which group is right? As is the case when trying to decide whether there are truly "poor" people or not, it is important for you to be able to recognize that neither view regarding the limited (or unlimited) nature of wealth is truly "right"; neither view represents the "Great Truth".

Instead, due to the paradoxical nature of wealth, each view simply appears to be "right" from a certain perspective, but neither view can ever appear to be "right" from all possible perspectives. Maybe the following thought experiment will help make this a little clearer.

Let us assume that you have an infinite piece of land to build a house on. Let us further assume that you have an unlimited amount of resources available to build your house. Since there are no limits to the size of house you can build, you decide to build a house of unlimited size.

In one sense, we could easily describe your house as being unlimited because it is constantly growing in size and there are no limits to how big it will be. But on the other hand, if we look at your house at any moment in time, your house will always be a specific size at that specific moment, so it will in fact be limited.

This is how wealth works. Even though it is constantly being created and there is no limit to how much can be created, at any specific moment in time there will always be a limited amount of wealth available to everyone. So, if a small percentage of the population decides to keep a majority of the wealth that currently exists for themselves, they will in fact be preventing the others from having as much wealth **at that moment in time**.

Of course, this is not true for any new wealth generated by the economy. Any new wealth created by the economy is free to go to anyone. So, in theory, the people who are currently poor are free to capture the new wealth for themselves, therefore they are free to improve their own economic well-being.

However, as we shall see, the act of truly "creating" wealth is not nearly as easy as many people seem to think. In addition, the economic beliefs that we have chosen to believe in make it exceedingly unlikely that any new wealth generated by our economy will find its way to the poor.

But for now, we just need to be able to recognize that issues such as whether people are truly "poor" or not, or whether wealth is truly unlimited or not, are really not all that interesting (or even all that important) since there is no truly "right" answer in either case. Due to the paradoxical nature of wealth, one can easily get locked into an unending philosophical debate on these subjects; and while you may enjoy pointless, long-winded discussions, I do not.

Therefore, I am going to focus the rest of this book on issues that are more interesting (and more important). We are going to focus our attention on trying to understand **why wealth is distributed the way that it is** and **the effect that this distribution has on the economy**. As we shall see, there are many people in this country who believe very strongly in some very naïve ideas regarding economics and it is these naïve ideas that are holding our economy back.

Myth 2: Life is a Competition

It may seem a little counter-intuitive, but to truly understand economics, one cannot simply study economics. You must also work very hard at understanding how ideas from other disciplines shape our views on economics.

Unfortunately for all of us, most economists are so busy studying economics, that they generally don't bother studying the ideas from other disciplines. They seem to operate under the delusion that the ideas from fields like biology, physics, religion, etc., have no direct bearing on our economic beliefs. This type of narrow-minded view of the world helps to explain why so many economists believe in so many profoundly flawed ideas regarding economic activity.

For example, by failing to understand the process of natural selection, many people (including economists and general citizens alike) have been fooled into thinking that life is a constant struggle where organisms compete with one another for precious resources. Because of this, people will often compete with each other even if it is not in their best interest to do so.

What we need to understand is that life often appears to be a competition simply because there is no formal mechanism in place to establish which organisms should succeed and which ones should not. Without some type of external structure to define their behavior, individual organisms are essentially forced to try and lead their lives using only their own limited concept of reality.

In general, each organism on this planet does its best to succeed in life; each organism essentially tries to do "good" according to its own concept of reality. The problem is that each organism has such a limited concept of reality, they invariably wind up pursuing ideas that prove to be harmful to other entities.

So, for example, tigers do not stalk and kill their prey because that is the way life must be. Tigers are essentially forced to stalk and kill their prey **because they are too stupid to figure out a better way to get food**. If tigers could figure out a strategy for finding food that was more universally beneficial, they would do so in a heartbeat. But they can't, **because they are idiots**.

If we take a "big picture" look at life here on Earth, we can see that we live on a planet that is populated by billions of idiots all running loose with no universal set of rules to keep them in line. It should be obvious to you that in such a situation there is naturally going to be a lot of conflict.

It should also be rather obvious to you that if we continue to believe in the naïve idea that life is a competition, **if we continue to justify our own behavior by the lessons we have learned from observing the behavior of a bunch of complete idiots**, then our future certainly looks less than promising.

We seem to be the only species on this planet that has a chance to do something about this situation. We seem to be the only ones capable of recognizing **why** other organisms are forced to compete with one another and can therefore possibly move beyond such a naïve view of the world.

Myth 3: You too can be Rich!

We already saw in the first myth that it is impossible for us to truly define what it means to be "poor" or "rich". However, the belief that anybody can be rich if they are just willing to work hard enough has become so entrenched in our society, I feel that it is necessary for us to at least briefly address the issue.

The myth that great wealth is just sitting out there waiting for you to take it is obviously a natural byproduct of the first two myths we discussed. Unfortunately, the competition for wealth guarantees us a world where most people will fail in their efforts to become rich and it is easy to see why this is the case.

Which is more important to our economy, gold or air? Clearly air is more important than gold. After all, without air nothing else even matters.

Which is more valuable in our economy, gold or air? Clearly gold is more valuable. After all, it trades for well over $1,000 per ounce as of this writing, while air is generally free.

*So why is it that the resource that is far and away the **most important** is also far and away the **least valuable**?* This little exercise highlights what economists often refer to as the Paradox of Value; the title of which makes no sense whatsoever since there is no paradox.

In order to understand why this is the case, we need to first understand that all of economic activity is based on "trade". When I get a job, I am "trading" my labor for wages. I give my labor to the company and in exchange the company gives me wages.

When I receive my paycheck, I go out and "trade" my wages for goods and services. I give some of my wages to the bartender and the bartender gives me some beer.

Thus, the only things in our economy that are going to have any **economic value** are those things that have **trade value.** Therefore, air has no economic value because it has no trade value; and it has no trade value because everyone already has it. I am not willing to trade you anything for some air because I already have as much air as I need.

Of course, the same goes for all economic entities (gold, stocks, bonds, money, etc.). If a company issued an infinite amount of stock, its per share price would drop to zero. If the US decided to print an infinite amount of dollars, the value of a dollar would drop to zero. If we could mine an unlimited amount of gold, then gold would become worthless.

So, the only way to be "rich" (in economic terms) is to own more things of economic value than other people have; and the only things that are going to hold any economic value are those things that are in limited supply.

Not surprisingly, since we mistakenly view life as being a competition, people naturally feel that we should compete over who gets to possess the wealth we create. To help us understand how this competition for wealth inevitably leads to a concentration of wealth into the hands of a few individuals, let us use the National Football League (NFL) as a simple analogy.

In the NFL a win is essentially a form of wealth. Wins are quite valuable because at the end of the regular season, the eight teams that have collected the most wins by division make it into the playoffs; plus, the two non-divisional winners in each conference with the most wins get into the playoffs as a "wild card". These twelve playoff teams then compete to see who gets to possess the ultimate form of wealth in the NFL: The Super Bowl trophy.

At the other end of the economic scale, the team with the fewest wins during the regular season is deemed to have finished last and is "rewarded" with the first pick in the player draft for the following year; supposedly to help them create more wealth (i.e. wins) in the future.

Let us assume that before the start of the next season **every player in the league** decides that they are just going to have fun and not try very hard the entire season. They plan to go out drinking with friends every night and skip every practice, but they will still play in the games each week. After all, the games are the fun part of the season! *What do think would happen?*

Well, the play would be pretty sloppy during the regular season, but at the end of the year, twelve teams would still make it into the playoffs and one of those teams would eventually wind up winning the Super Bowl. Also, some team would still finish with the worst record in the league and would get the first pick in the following year's draft. In other words, regardless of the level of play during the year, the reward profile will still be essentially the same at the end of the year.

Now let us assume that after one year of just goofing around, **all the players on one team** (let us say that it is the Miami Dolphins) decide to work very hard the following year, while the rest of the players in the league continue goofing around. The Dolphins do not go out drinking with friends and they make it to every single practice session. Because they are so much better prepared to play football, they wind up being the Super Bowl champion at the end of the year. From this, many people would reach the naïve conclusion that all it takes is hard work for one to succeed in life.

To see why this is not the case, let us assume that the following year **every player in the league** decides to work very hard. They all quit drinking and they all make it to every single practice session. *Would they all win the Super Bowl*? Of course not. At the end of the year twelve teams would make the playoffs, one team would become Super Bowl champion and one team would still finish in last place

The point to recognize here is that the level of effort of the participants would clearly affect the quality of play in the league, but it would not affect the distribution of the rewards at the end of the year. No matter how hard each participant tries (or doesn't try), the reward profile will essentially be the same. The same number of teams will always make the playoffs, there will only be one Super Bowl winner and one poor team will *always* come in last place.

We can see a similar outcome in an economic system. The level of effort of each member will determine the overall material state of the system (i.e. it will determine the total amount of wealth available in the system), but the wealth will always wind up accumulating into only a few hands as long as the goal of each member is to become rich.

The only way to become "rich" is to possess items of economic value. The only things that will have any economic value are those things that are in limited supply. Thus, it is physically impossible for everyone to become "rich", because if everyone figured out a way to get their hands on some item of economic value, the trade value of that item would plummet.

It is important to note that much has been written lately about the growing divide between the rich and the poor in this country, but most of these writings are extremely misleading in that they always seem to blame only the rich people for the divide. To the contrary, as we will see in the next two chapters, the divide is actually the result of **everyone** trying to keep wealth for themselves; and the harder **everyone** tries to get "rich", the wider the wealth divide will naturally become.

Myth 4: Low Prices are Good for America

Another way to further learn about the effects of competition on the income distribution here in the US is to look at one of the benchmarks of competitive behavior: Wal-Mart. Wal-Mart has spent a lot of time and money in an effort to portray itself as a champion of competitive efficiency. They have made it a concerted point to train the American consumer into thinking that low prices are good for America and that they are some sort of American hero because they provide these low prices to consumers.

Unfortunately, much of this is simply not true. One critical component of economic activity that you need to recognize is that **price levels are purely symbolic reflections of the decisions made by the market participants**. Because they are purely symbolic, prices are pretty much irrelevant if we take a "big picture" view of the economy. This may sound strange, but it is a relatively easy matter to see why this is the case.

Let us assume that you buy item X from Wal-Mart every week and it typically sells for $5.00. Now let us further assume that Wal-Mart decides to lower the price to $4.00. *Is this a **universally** "good" thing*?

You might be tempted to say "Well, of course it is. I just saved myself $1.00 per week!" Yes, **you** save $1.00 per week, but now Wal-Mart is going to receive $1.00 **less** per week from you, so the price cut was a wash if we look at the big picture; your $1.00 "gain" was offset by Wal-Mart's $1.00 "loss".

Or maybe it would become clearer if you think about it this way, let us assume that you sell pumpkins for $5.00 each and I want to buy one from you. *How would you change the price of the pumpkin so that the resulting change would be "good for America"?*

It should be obvious to you that it is impossible to do so. No matter which direction we move the price, as good as the change is for one of us, that change will always be equally bad for the other.

> *So, if the idea of low prices being "good for America" is so obviously not true, how is it that so many people seem to believe so strongly in it?*

Due to our poor educational system, combined with the overwhelmingly complicated nature of our economy, we are simply not capable of recognizing how our purchase decisions impact the economy as a whole and our own personal economy.

As was mentioned earlier, our current educational system is much too "fact" based. Such a system does not give people the ability to use logic and reason correctly; thus, we are easily fooled into believing: *"If a lower price is good for me and I am a part of the economy, then the lower price must be good for the economy!"*

While most economists may not fall for such simple-minded logic, they do fall victim to a similar line of thinking. Because they don't bother to study other disciplines such as physics, they fail to understand that the world can take on a very different meaning depending upon the perspective from which it is measured.

Economists are so focused on finding the "Great Truth" about economics (which doesn't exist), that they are easily misled into only looking at the economy from a single perspective. We will talk about this in more detail in Myth 13, but for now you just need to be aware that economists easily lose sight of the difference between looking at the economy from a **business perspective** versus looking at the economy from an **economic perspective**.

Looking at the world from a **business perspective** only requires you to look at the world from a singular perspective. That is, you only need to look at the world from the perspective of one business, one household, one individual, etc. In each of these cases, **income and expenses are separate from each other;** and are in fact opposites.

So, if you are a baker and the price of flour goes up, then that is "bad" for your business because your expenses just went up. On the other hand, if you can raise the price of the bread that you sell, then that is "good" because your income just went up.

In contrast, when you are looking at the world from an **economic perspective**, you always have to look at the world from multiple perspectives. From the standpoint of the economy as a whole, **there are always two sides to every price tag**. On one side of the price tag you have income to the seller and on the other side of the price tag you have an expense for the buyer. Thus, in Economics: **Expenses = Income** (or if you prefer, **Spending = Income**).

So, from an economic perspective, if the price of flour goes up, it will be bad for the baker, but good for the flour maker. If the price of bread goes up, it will be good for the baker, but bad for the consumer.

Here it is critical for you to be able to recognize that due to their two-sided nature, prices end up acting much like a thermometer for our economy. If you are a doctor examining a patient, a thermometer can provide you with very useful information about the patient, **but it will not directly affect the health of the patient**. That is to say that a thermometer is not going to make the patient sicker or healthier.

Similarly, prices can provide us with very useful information about the forces at work in the economy, **but they do not drive the economy**. So lower prices are not "good" or "bad" for the economy and higher prices are not "good" or "bad" for the economy. The different price levels simply relay information to us about what forces are at work within the economy; but they do not make the economy sicker or healthier.

> *Wait a minute, why in the world would a company like Wal-Mart do something that is "**bad**" for **them**? Why would they cut their prices if it means that they will take in **less** money for each item they sell?*

A company like Wal-Mart is willing to cut their prices because they know that in the long run it will allow them to exert more leverage on the economic system in general.

By training consumers to be so price sensitive, big businesses have made it extremely difficult for small businesses to compete with them. Small businesses cannot generate large enough economies of scale; therefore, they cannot offer the same low prices that big business can.

By consistently driving down prices, big businesses have been able to reduce the number of small businesses in the economy. This has reduced the amount of competition that big businesses face, which has allowed big businesses to make large profits while still maintaining relatively low prices.

In addition, by reducing the amount of competition they face, Wal-Mart is able to attract more shoppers to their stores (by offering consumers the low prices that the consumers have been trained to look for). By attracting more consumers to their stores, Wal-Mart is then able to go to its suppliers and say "We are the biggest outlet in the world for your goods. If you want me to continue selling your goods in my stores, you need to lower the price of the goods that you supply to me."

The supplier has little choice but to meet Wal-Mart's demands. The supplier could try and sell its goods to another store, such as Target or Kmart, but those stores are busy trying to keep up with Wal-Mart and are under pressure to lower their costs as well.

This pressure to lower costs has run its way through the entire supply chain and has forced businesses of all sizes to eliminate costs wherever possible. One very positive outcome from all this pressure is that businesses have been forced to make their production and distribution systems much more efficient, which has been a boon to the economy.

But on the negative side, this pressure has also led business leaders to ship labor intensive jobs overseas, hold down wages wherever possible, force workers to pay for more of their own healthcare, cut other benefits and increase the use of part-time workers, all in an effort to meet the cost demands brought on by the consumer's insatiable desire for low prices.

Not so long ago, workers used to join unions as a means of protecting their economic interests, but big business has done a fantastic job of portraying unions as being cumbersome and wasteful entities that make it impossible for a company to stay competitive in a dynamic marketplace. Unions have essentially been portrayed as being "anti-American" because they prevent companies from offering the consumer the low prices that the consumer so desperately wants.

Not surprisingly, unions have lost a tremendous amount of leverage on our economic system during the last sixty years. In 1948, union membership as a percentage of the total workforce stood at 31.8%. By 2009, it was down to 12.3% (per the Department of Labor).

Wal-Mart in particular has waged a calculated campaign against anyone who has tried to unionize their workforce, because if unions were to move into Wal-Mart, the employees would gain leverage on the system and could demand better wages and benefits. This would disrupt Wal-Mart's ability to offer low prices to the consumer which of course is the key to their ability to exert more leverage on the economic system in general.

The point to recognize from all of this is that Wal-Mart is able to recover the $1.00 that they "lose" from lowering their price on item X by both reducing the amount of competition they face and by extracting cost savings from their suppliers and employees. And of course, the suppliers to Wal-Mart turn around and do the same thing to their suppliers and employees, thus putting even more strain on the system; particularly on the wages paid to working people.

What has made the overall process so effective is that the average consumer simply does not possess a sufficient enough understanding of economics to be able to see the impact that their purchasing decision has on the distribution of wealth in this country. They just figure, "*Hey, I might as well save myself a couple bucks where I can.*" What they cannot see is that the money they "save" by looking for lower prices is, in many cases, actually coming out of their own pocket.

*But haven't consumers **always** wanted lower
prices? Why is the income gap only showing up now?*

In order to understand why this is the case, we need to briefly examine the evolution of the consumer. If you look at a very poor person slaving away in a rice field struggling just to make a living, it should be obvious to you that almost all his income goes toward satisfying his "needs". He is simply not productive enough to allow him to spend much of his income on any fanciful "wants". He is, in the truest sense of the word, a "consumer" because he typically consumes all his income.

Here in America, due to the effects of specialization, we have been able to raise our productivity to the point where the amount of our income that goes towards satisfying true "needs" is very, very small. Instead, the vast majority of our purchases are for things we merely "want". Because of this, most Americans can afford to be much choosier than the poor rice farmer as to when, where and at what price they are going to buy the majority of their goods.

In short, the typical American can now afford to spend a lot of time and energy trying to minimize the price they pay for the goods they buy. Thus, the typical American is no longer a true "consumer" but is instead a "**profit maximizer**".

That is to say that the typical American behaves more like a corporation than like the poor person slaving away in the rice field. The typical American will try to maximize their income, minimize the cost of the goods they buy and, if possible, stash away as much "profit" as they can.

Of course, on some level, consumers have always **wanted** to behave this way. However, they never truly had the power to do so until the advent of globalization, the proliferation of the automobile and the expansion of the internet.

By breaking down trade barriers, globalization has allowed relatively cheap goods to flood into our economy; giving consumers a seemingly infinite amount of choices as to what they are going to consume. The infinite amount of choices in front of them allows the consumer to "play each business against one another". If one particular company can't offer a low enough price, consumers can simply look for another company that will, either by driving across town or by shopping the seemingly unlimited number of retail sites on the internet.

Due to all the downward pressure on prices (**which is coming from rich people and poor people alike**), businesses have been forced to do everything they can to lower their prices (or at least keep them from rising). Naturally, if they are going to lower/maintain their prices they are also going to have to lower/maintain their costs in order to make a profit. Not surprisingly, our corporations have become obsessed with controlling costs; and of course, one of the largest costs in most corporations comes in the form of wages.

So now our overall economic situation becomes clearer. Every individual and corporation in this country is basically trying to maximize their "profits". To achieve this goal, they are all pushing down on prices/costs as hard as they can. In doing so, they are unwittingly pushing down as hard as they can on the wages of the working class, thus making it virtually impossible for wages to keep pace with productivity (*as we saw in figure 2 in the Introduction*).

Maybe the following example can help make our situation a little clearer. Let us say that company AAA has been paying its workers $10.00 per hour and they have been producing 4 units per hour, so their labor cost per unit is $2.50. In addition, let us further assume that their total unit cost per item is $3.50 and that they have been selling item Y for $5.00 per unit.

Now let us assume that they figure out a way to redesign their production process so that they can make 5 units per hour instead of the usual 4. Because of this productivity improvement, their labor unit cost would drop to $2.00 and their total unit cost would drop to $3.00. Since their cost per unit just went down, company AAA basically has four options available to them.

Option 1: they could choose to keep the unit price and the workers' wages the same. In this case all the value of the productivity improvement would go to the owners of company AAA in the form of additional profit per item sold.

Option 2: they could choose to keep the price the same but raise the workers' wages to $12.50 per hour. In this case all the value of the productivity improvement would go to the workers.

Option 3: they could choose to keep the workers' wages the same but lower the unit price by $.50. In this case all the value of the productivity improvement would go to the consumers.

Option 4: the company could choose to do some combination of the first three options. (e.g. they could lower the price by $.10, raise wages by $.50 and let the rest go to the owners as profit; or they could lower the price by $.40 and let the rest go to the owners; etc.)

Due to the fact that most people in this country have chosen to believe in the extremely naïve idea that life is a competition, anytime that new wealth is introduced into the economy (through a productivity improvement), people will naturally compete to see which of the above options actually gets chosen. So, the owners will do all that they can to try and get Option 1 chosen, the workers will do all that they can to see that Option 2 gets chosen, and the consumers will do all that they can to see that Option 3 gets chosen. Not surprisingly, the outcome of this competition will ultimately be determined by who can exert the most leverage over the decision: owners, workers or consumers.

As we have already seen, the evolution of the consumer into a "profit maximizer", has given consumers a tremendous amount of leverage in this competition. So, they have naturally been the biggest winners in this competition.

Conversely, these factors have all conspired to significantly reduce the amount of leverage that workers have in the competition. Thus, the wages for the working class have lagged far behind the rate of productivity growth in our economy for the past several decades (*as we saw in figure 2*).

While the consumer has been the biggest gainer, owners have also made some impressive gains in the competition for wealth. It is worth noting that corporate profits initially fell as cheaper foreign goods started flowing into the US economy in the mid to late 1970s. Since then, however, American businesses have focused intensely on controlling costs; the result being a relatively steady increase in corporate profits as a percentage of GDP since the early 1980s: (Figure 6)

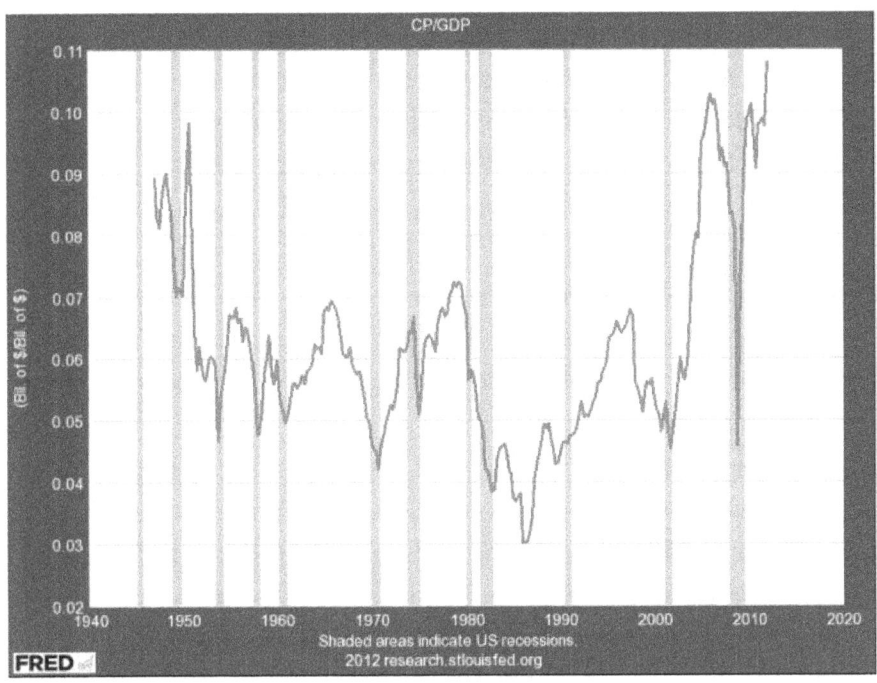

Shaded areas indicate US recessions.
2012 research.stlouisfed.org

One of the main reasons that owners have been able to achieve these gains, despite the consumer's intense pressure on prices, is the fact that there are many individuals in this country who naively believe that corporations should solely focus on maximizing profits. These people mistakenly believe that any increase in corporate profitability will ultimately be good for the economy because the corporation will always look to invest those profits back into the economy. As we will see in the next chapter, this is simply not true.

For now, we just need to recognize that the consumer's naïve desire for low prices, coupled with the effects of globalization, have created a system in which it is almost impossible for the wages of the working class to keep up with productivity. In fact, it is easy to see that our naïve economic beliefs have created a vicious circle.

Consumers naively demand lower prices. Businesses are then forced to aggressively control costs in order to deliver lower prices to consumers. Workers feel the downward pressure on their wages, so they naturally become concerned about their financial situation. Therefore, they try even harder to save money on the goods they buy. This unwittingly puts even more pressure on their own wages, which makes them even more concerned about their financial situation. So, they try even harder to save money on the goods they buy; and the circle continues.

Since the wages of the working class are trapped under all the downward pressure on prices, any new wealth introduced into the economy is always going to flow to the top. So, the rich get richer and the poor get poorer. The weakest participants in our economy continually "lose" because they cannot exert any leverage on the system. Naturally this means that the strongest participants in the economy continually "win"; thus creating the increasing wealth divide that we have witnessed over the past several decades.

Of course, many people see no problem with this; they feel that this is the way that life should be. After all, life is a competition; the strongest and smartest should get all the rewards.

On the other hand, there are also some people who still cling to the belief that "as you did to one of the least of these my brothers, you did to me." They cling to the belief that it isn't "fair" to have a system where the same people continually reap all the benefits.

So, who is right? Again, due to the paradoxical nature of wealth, there is no truly "right" answer. Neither view represents the "Great Truth" about our economy. Each view is entirely subjective and will only appeal to specific groups of people. As we saw earlier in our story about the fairy giving wealth to only half of the inhabitants of an island nation, rich people will tend to support the views that favor rich people and poor people will tend to support the views that favor poor people.

The critical thing to recognize here is that the argument over whether our economic system is "fair" is in many ways pointless because neither side is truly "right". So instead of wasting our time on an argument that has no truly "right" answer, we need to focus our attention on the fact that **by not allowing the wages of the working class to keep pace with productivity, we are helping to create some very serious problems for our economy**.

There is a basic concept within economics referred to as the Marginal Propensity to Consume (MPC). Simply put, it is a measure of how much of one's income is going to be consumed. So, if I gave you $100 and you spent $75 and you saved the remaining $25, we would say that your MPC was 75% and that your Marginal Propensity to Save (MPS) was 25%.

In general, as an individual's income rises, their MPC tends to fall; conversely their MPS naturally increases. So, if you gave $100 to a poor person and $100 to a rich person, the poor person would generally spend more of the $100 than the rich person. *Why is this important?*

As we mentioned earlier, by having everyone push down on prices as hard as they can, we have created a system in which the poor always "lose" and the rich always "win". Thus, we find ourselves stuck in an endless cycle. As the new wealth generated by productivity improvements keeps going to those people in our economy that are already wealthy, **our overall MPC keeps declining**.

This process has been underway for decades. As we will see in Myth 6, the net result of this is that we now have trillions of dollars of savings "sitting on the sidelines" waiting to be invested in the economy, but nowhere to invest that money **due to a lack of aggregate demand**.

For now, we just need to be able to recognize that many people have recognized the growing wealth divide in this country and automatically jumped to the mistaken conclusion that our economic system must be "broken" or "rigged". The critical point that these people have failed to recognize is that the problem is not with our economic **system**; the problem is with our economic **beliefs**.

The growing wealth divide is a natural result of **everyone** pushing down on prices as hard as they can. This makes it impossible for wages to track productivity, which lowers the aggregate demand in our economy, which makes it financially imprudent to invest in the productive assets that we need to grow our economy. So, the next time that you hear some economic *"expert"* touting lower prices as being "good for the economy", you will know that you are listening to a complete idiot.

Myth 5: Main Goal is to Maximize Profits

This myth was first introduced by one of the most influential and celebrated economists of all time: Milton Friedman. Many people assume that since the idea came from such a seemingly important economist, surely the idea must be true. Sadly, nothing could be further from the truth.

As I mentioned earlier, most economists are morons because they do not bother to study anything other than economics. Because they do not study disciplines like philosophy and physics, they ignorantly believe that the economy is much like a giant game of billiards or chess where all the entities can move independently of one another.

In reality, since there are two sides to every price tag, the economy is more akin to physics; where the movement of any one entity directly influences all other entities. Every dollar of expense for one entity is a dollar of income for somebody else.

As we discussed in the previous chapter, each segment of our economy (owner, worker, customer) is currently in a misguided competition to see how many dollars they can possess. Not surprisingly, each segment will inevitably gravitate towards any ideas that help give it the strength to grab as many dollars as possible.

Thus, the owners in our economy adopted Friedman's ideas, not because those ideas were part of the "Great Truth" of economics, but because those ideas helped to give the owners the strength to grab more dollars for themselves. As I have said before, people have an unerring tendency to believe in ideas that are ideally suited to their own personal experience with the world.

It is interesting to note that the idea that businesses should focus on maximizing profits really didn't take hold in this country until the late 1970s; and didn't really become an obsession until the mid-1980s. Looking at figures 1 and 6, we can see that since corporations have become so focused on profits, the economy has been gradually getting weaker and at the same time, corporate profits as a percentage of GDP have been rising rather dramatically.

In fact, corporate profits are now at an all-time high and at the same time the economy is still fundamentally weak. Anyone with half an ounce of intelligence should be able to recognize that increasing corporate profits is clearly not the way to improve the health of the economy. After all, *if record profits haven't turned the economy around, what do we need? Extra-special, super profits?*

Now, for us to truly appreciate the absurdity of this myth, we need to examine it from several different perspectives. First of all, regardless of what the Supreme Court may say, we need to understand that not only are corporations not people, they are not even actual entities. Corporations are nothing more than a "**legal fiction**". As such, they do not have goals or rights or hopes or dreams.

Of course, corporations are owned and staffed by individuals that are bound to each other through the legal arrangement known as a corporation. And of course, each of the individuals within this legal framework has their own goals, rights, hopes and dreams, but the legal arrangement itself (i.e. the corporation) does not.

Giving corporations their own goals is intellectually equivalent to giving a "marriage" goals that are somehow separate from the individuals getting married. Imagine going to dinner at your friend's house and he says "I would like you to meet my wife, Amy, and I would also like you to meet my marriage. Amy and I are hoping to take a trip to Hawaii next year, but our marriage really wants to go to Bali."

As ridiculous as that conversation sounds, the idea that a corporation's "main goal is to maximize profits" is just as ridiculous. Imagine taking a tour at IBM and hearing "I would like you to meet our CEO and our janitor; and I would also like you to meet IBM. The CEO and janitor would each like a pay raise, but IBM wants to cut their wages in order to increase profits."

Secondly, even if we make the ignorant assumption that corporations are actual entities with their own rights and goals, it should be readily obvious to you that profit "maximization" is still not the appropriate "main" goal of the corporation. After all, consider what would happen if we went to each individual within a corporation and asked them if they would like a 10% pay raise. *How many people do you think would turn the raise down* **because they would be afraid that it would reduce the profitability of the corporation**?

Unless the corporation was on the verge of bankruptcy, I can pretty much guarantee you that it would be exactly zero. Therefore, not a single person in our corporations is truly focused on what is supposedly the "main goal" of the corporation.

So why do we focus on maximizing profits?

First of all, as I mentioned earlier, most people are not capable of seeing the world from multiple perspectives.

Because of this, they mistakenly believe that running an economy is essentially the same as running a business. Since the economy is full of businesses, they mistakenly believe that if something is good for one business, then it must be good for the economy as a whole since that business is a part of the economy.

After all, if company BBB increases its profits, then its value as a firm goes up. *If the value of company BBB goes up, doesn't the value of the entire economic system go up as well*? So, to maximize the value of our economy as a whole, each company should simply focus on maximizing its own value. *If every company maximizes their own value, won't the value of the whole system necessarily be maximized*?

The answer to each of these questions is a resounding NO. As I mentioned in Myth 3, if everybody has something, then it becomes worthless in economic terms. So, the only way for a company to "maximize" its own value is to keep things of value for itself (i.e. **to try and keep things of value away from other companies/individuals**). To see why I say this, let us assume that Keith works for company BBB. Keith earns $10.00 per hour and makes 4 hammers per hour. Let us further assume that the hammers sell for $15.00 each.

Now let us assume that company BBB cuts Keith's wages to $8.00 per hour and that he continues producing 4 hammers per hour. In this instance, BBB's profits would go up due to the lower cost of Keith's wages; thus, the value of BBB would go up as well. But no additional wealth would have been created because Keith would still be producing the same $60.00 of wealth per hour.

The key point here is that by cutting Keith's wages, BBB made it impossible for Keith to be able to support the same amount of other businesses as he was able to when he was earning $10.00 per hour. By lowering Keith's wages, BBB was indirectly lowering the revenue of other companies; **so, the increase in the value of BBB came at the expense of those other companies**. This is why cost cutting measures do not make the economy any better. They simply rearrange the wealth that already exists in the economy.

Wait a minute! Couldn't the owners of BBB simply use their increased profits to support the businesses that Keith can no longer support?

Yes, they **could**, if they chose to **spend** those profits. But as we saw in Myth 4, an individual's MPC tends to go down as one's income goes up. So, by shifting the income away from Keith (the working class) and to the owners (the wealthy), we inevitably increase the amount of income that is saved in this country; thus the profits are not fully consumed.

In addition, by mistakenly believing in the idea that businesses should seek to maximize their own value, businesses are inevitably led to retain their profits in an effort to drive up their own stock price. This short-sighted behavior is then defended by many so-called economic *"experts"* in this country who ignorantly claim that businesses are just "keeping their powder dry" until the economy turns around.

What these *"experts"* fail to understand is that **the act of saving** (including retaining earnings) is preventing the economy from turning around; we will discuss this in more detail in the next chapter.

The second main reason that people mistakenly believe that businesses should maximize their profits is the mistaken belief that profits are the primary reason that businesses are formed; this is also not true.

As hard as it may be for you to believe, the simple fact of the matter is that we **DO NOT** form businesses in order to make money. We form businesses because doing so allows us to produce goods and services in a far more efficient manner than we could otherwise hope to achieve on our own.

If you were forced to provide your own food, housing, clothing, medical care, etc., you would struggle just to stay alive. No matter how hard you tried, you would never get to be as good at building a house as somebody who did nothing but build houses all day. You would never get to be as good at growing food as somebody who did nothing but grow food all day. You would never get to be as good at providing healthcare as somebody who did nothing but provide healthcare all day. So, if you were forced to try and provide solely for yourself, you would wind up living in a crappy house; eating crappy food; getting crappy medical attention; etc.

In contrast, by living in a society with organized businesses, it is possible for each of us to focus solely on specific tasks that need to be done within our economy. You may simply need to sell computers all day, or maybe just clean office buildings all day, or maybe just oversee the production of a new factory, or any of the millions of other tasks that need to be done in order to provide ourselves with the goods and services we desire.

There is no need for you to know how to fix a car, grow corn, treat chicken pox, etc. There are other people in the economy who will focus on the tasks that lead to the completion of those projects. You simply need to focus on being the best that you can be at whatever task you are hired to do.

Because each of us is able to focus our efforts solely on the completion of a very specific task, we are generally able to become very proficient at that task (which is just another way of saying that we are able to become much more productive).

And, as we will see in Myth 9, the more productive that each member of a society becomes, the more wealth that will be available to the society as a whole.

So, by helping to increase the productivity of each member of society, businesses are capable of enriching our lives and dramatically increasing our economic well-being. From all of this, you should be able to recognize that the real "main goal" of any business is the same as the main goal of **all economic participants**, which is **to become more productive**.

In order to help drive this point home, let us return to our earlier example. Let us once again assume that Keith works for BBB, makes 4 hammers per hour, gets paid $10.00 per hour and the hammers sell for $15.00.

Let us further assume that they figure out a way to redesign their production process so that Keith is now able to produce 5 hammers per hour. Under this scenario, Keith is now able to produce $75 of wealth per hour; thus, the total amount of wealth in the economy just went up.

As we saw in the previous chapter, this new wealth can either be passed on to Keith in the form of higher wages, to the owners in the form of higher profits, to the customers in the form of lower prices or some combination of the three. Let us assume that BBB decides to keep Keith's wages and the price of the hammers the same; so, all of the value of the productivity improvement goes to the owners in the form of higher profits.

In this case, the value of BBB would naturally rise due to their increased profitability and at the same time Keith would still be able to support the same amount of other businesses. In this case the overall economy would be larger because BBB's gain did not come at anyone else's expense.

Here it is absolutely critical for you to recognize that the economy grew **because of the productivity improvement**; **NOT** because of the increase in profits.

I suppose that it is also worth pointing out that if we simply raised Keith's wages to $12.00 per hour, while he was still only producing 4 hammers per hour, BBB's profits would go down, thus its value would go down. But Keith would be able to support more businesses on his higher salary, so the value of those other businesses would go up. Again, there would be no change in the total amount of wealth in the system. BBB's loss in value would simply be gained by the other businesses that Keith supports.

The point being that simply raising wages is not "good" for the economy for the same reason that simply lowering wages is not "good" for the economy. In each case, you are not **creating** any wealth; you are just shifting the existing amount of wealth around.

Similarly, raising profits isn't "good" for the economy for the same reason that lowering profits isn't "good" for the economy. All you are doing is pushing costs around and this has no impact on productivity; which is what really drives the economy. If you simply push costs around, one company's profits will always come at the expense of the other stakeholders to that business (i.e. its employees, its consumers, the economy at large, etc.).

What we need to recognize from all of this is that the problem with our economy is not that wages have not gone up; **the problem is that wages have not kept up with productivity, which has been rising**. And of course, the reason why wages have not kept up with productivity is due to the effects of the ignorant beliefs that "Low Prices are Good for America" and "Main Goal of a Business is to Maximize Profits".

How would a business maximize its profits? It would try and maximize its revenue while minimizing its costs. *How would it minimize its costs?* In part, by minimizing its number of employees and their wages. Gee, I wonder why we have so many employment problems in this country!

As was referenced earlier, we have seen a dramatic increase in the number of people in this country who have been unemployed for longer than 52 weeks (*see figure 3*). The reason for this increase is the simple fact that from a business perspective, these people are too expensive. They have been out of work for so long, businesses are afraid it would cost too much to retrain them, thus it is very difficult for these people to find work.

In addition, we can see in figure 5 that it has taken us longer and longer for the job market to recover from each of the last four recessions. Again, this is partly due to the effects of the "employment minimization" that is a natural by-product of the ignorant belief that businesses should focus primarily on profits.

In order for the job market to truly recover, we are going to have to get people to realize that profits are merely a **means to an end**; they are not an end in themselves. Businesses need to be able to make a profit in order to be able to invest in the productive assets they need to help make their workers more productive (which is their real main goal!).

However, by focusing too much on profits (by individuals and businesses alike), we inevitably end up saving too much. In the next chapter we will see how this strips the economy of the demand needed to justify the investment into productive assets.

Of course, the ultimate irony here is that most people try to focus on profitability in the naïve belief that increasing profits will make us wealthier. What they cannot see is that by focusing on **profitability** instead of **productivity**, we actually guarantee that we will not be as wealthy as we otherwise could be.

To see why I say this, imagine there are two different planets. On planet 1 everyone spends 100% of their time trying to be more productive. On planet 2 people spend 100% of their time trying to be more profitable (i.e. trying to capture the wealth that already exists for themselves).

It should be obvious to you that the people on planet 1 are going to be more productive; therefore, they are going to produce more wealth; therefore, they are going to be wealthier. So, by wasting our time focusing on profitability, we create a world that contains less wealth than it otherwise could. Now that, Miss Morissette, is ironic!

A hundred years from now people will be shaking their heads in disbelief. They will have an extremely hard time understanding how so many people could believe so strongly in an idea that is so profoundly idiotic. The notion that chasing profits will lead to more wealth will seem as foreign to them as the idea that the moon is made of cheese.

Myth 6: Saving is Good for the Economy

This is one of those myths that has been handed down from generation to generation and has become so engrained into the American psyche that to even suggest that saving is not good for the economy is almost considered to be heresy. Part of the reason why this myth has become such a sacred part of our economic landscape is the simple fact that there are many people who do not seem to truly understand what the word "saving" actually means.

From an economic perspective, "**saving**" is simply the act of setting aside money to be used at a future time. So, if you take $5.00 and stick it in your wallet, that is "saving". If you take $5.00 and stick it in your mattress, that is "saving". If you take $5.00 and put it in the bank, that is "saving".

Of course, "**spending**" is simply the opposite of "saving". So, if you take the $5.00 out of your wallet and buy a bar of soap, that is "spending". If you take the $5.00 out of your mattress and buy a bit of gold, that is "spending". If you take the $5.00 out of your savings account at the bank and buy some stock in a soap company, that is "spending".

In today's world, it seems as though there are many people who mistakenly believe that buying stocks, bonds, gold, etc. is a form of saving; it is not. It is a form of spending often referred to as "investing"; which is simply the act of buying an asset in the hopes that its value will rise over time.

So, if you open up a 401k and have $100 withheld from your paycheck, we can say that you **saved** $100. At this point we could say that your savings balance is $100 and your investment balance is $0.

If the $100 is then used to **buy** shares in a mutual fund or **buy** shares of a specific stock or **buy** some other type of asset, we can then say that you **spent** your $100 in savings on an **investment**; so now your savings balance is $0 and your investment balance is $100.

Returning to our original discussion, we can now recognize that if you naively proclaim that "Saving is Good for the Economy", what you are also saying is that taking money and sticking it in a mattress is "good for the economy"; after all sticking money in a mattress is a form of "saving". So, according to your theory that "Saving is Good for the Economy", if everyone took all their money and stuck it in their mattress, the economy should take off like a rocket!

For your sake, I truly hope that I do not have to explain to you why sticking all our money in a mattress is not going to be good for the economy. Instead, you need to be able to recognize that **saving is actually very bad for the economy** (i.e. if everyone stuck all of their money in their mattress it would be very, very bad for the economy).

As I mentioned in Myth 4, Spending = Income. From this it shouldn't take a rocket scientist to figure out that Saving = No Income (since saving is the exact opposite of spending).

The sad thing about this is that economists have been fully aware of the harm done to the economy by saving for centuries (yes, centuries). The idea has even been formally given the unfortunate title of "Paradox of Thrift". I say unfortunate because it is no way, shape or form a paradox at all. It only appears to be a paradox to the millions of idiots who ignorantly believe that saving is good for the economy.

The idea should really be called "The Common Sense Result of Thrift" or "The Painfully Obvious Outcome of Thrift". To see why I say this, let us consider the following.

Let us assume there is an island economy where everyone spends 100% of their income. To make things easier to follow, let us say that there are 100 people on the island and they each make $1,000 a year; so, we can say that the annual demand in this economy is equal to $100,000 (= 100 * $1,000).

Now let us assume that a crazy witch doctor visits the island and convinces the islanders that saving is good for the economy. So everyone on the island decides to save 10% of their income; they each take $100 and stuff it into their mattress. Now we can see that each person in the economy is only going to be spending $900. Therefore, total demand (and total income) in the economy has fallen to $90,000 (= 100*$900). Clearly the saving was bad for the economy.

So, if saving is so clearly bad for the economy, then why do so many people think that it is good for the economy?

There are many reasons, but we will only focus on the three most important reasons. First of all, saving is clearly good for the saver. After all, if I manage to save $1,000,000, then I am clearly going to be in a much better financial position than someone who has no savings. So, there is a very strong incentive for savers to believe that "saving is good for the economy" because they want to believe that they are a "good person" who is doing "good things" for our economy.

As I have said repeatedly, people have an unerring tendency to believe in ideas that are ideally suited for their own personal experience with the world. Thus, a world full of savers is naturally going to be a world full of people who believe that saving is good for the economy.

Secondly, just as we cannot directly see the harm done to our economy by obsessing over lower prices, we cannot directly see the harm caused by the savings of any given individual or business. After all, if I stuff $1,000 into a mattress, I just saved $1,000 which is clearly good for me. Since our economy is so large, however, this small amount of saving won't even be noticed by anyone else. It wouldn't even qualify as a rounding error.

The harm caused by any act of saving gets spread out across the entire economy, so its impact on each individual economic participant is so small as to be unnoticeable. Therefore, the benefits of saving are crystal clear to the saver, but the harm it does to the economy is practically invisible.

In an economy in which the majority of participants save, the economy is constantly getting hurt by millions of tiny, tiny hits. Each hit to the economy is so small that it is unnoticeable, but in aggregate they are enough to have a noticeable effect on demand.

The third reason why people mistakenly believe that saving is good for the economy is due to the fact that it is possible for us to **use our savings** to do something that is very, **VERY** good for the economy. To see why I say this, let us return to our earlier story and assume that the islanders take the $10,000 that they saved and they invest it into a new factory that is able to produce $2,000 a year in income. Let us further assume that the islanders return to their original habit of not saving any of their income.

By spending the $10,000 they had originally saved, they restored demand back to its $100,000 level. In addition, they also now have the $2,000 in income from the new factory, so the total demand in their economy has now risen to $102,000; thus, their economy grew due to their wise investment. This is why many people are fooled into thinking that saving is good for the economy. If we invest (i.e. spend) our savings wisely, it is possible to grow our economy.

Unfortunately for all of us, there are many economists that mistakenly view the wise investment of our savings as being inevitable. Thus, they constantly harp that Americans need to save more in order to increase the amount of investment in our economy. As we continue our discussion, however, we will be able to see that our ignorant beliefs about the nature of saving work to prevent the investment of our savings.

Before we go any further, however, we need to take a moment and recognize that there are basically two different types of assets that we can invest our savings into: productive assets and non-productive assets.

Productive assets, as the name implies, are assets that are used in the production of goods and services. Some common examples are: tools, machinery, computers, buildings, training, etc. We invest in these assets whenever we want to **produce** something of value.

Non-productive assets, on the other hand, are things like stocks, bonds, gold, fine art, etc. These assets are held purely for their own intrinsic value; they are not capable of actually producing anything else of value.

Sadly, there are many people in this country who mistakenly believe that stocks and bonds are productive assets. It should be obvious that stocks and bonds are merely financing vehicles; however, due to our ineffective educational system, many people seem to be completely incapable of understanding this.

Let us assume that I am starting my own business where I intend to build the world's first electric kite. I convince a group of investors to buy $1,000,000,000 worth of stock in my company. I then spend the next year laying on the couch looking for a decent movie on Netflix. In this case, it should be painfully obvious to you that the $1,000,000,000 investment in the stock of my company has done absolutely nothing to help grow the economy.

As was mentioned before, and as will be explained in more detail in our discussion of Myth 9, the best way to grow the economy is to increase our productivity. From this, it shouldn't take a rocket scientist to figure out that the best way to increase our productivity is to invest in things that are going to make us more productive (duh!). That is, we need to invest in productive assets.

So, if I had used the $1,000,000,000 in proceeds from the stock sale to buy a factory, fill it with machines and hire some workers, then the economy would have grown. But it is critical for you to recognize that **it was the investment in these productive assets** and NOT the stock sale that caused the economy to grow.

Now, in order for us to be able to invest in productive assets, we clearly need to have some savings available. **This is where many people become confused because of their inability to use logic correctly.**

Because they are so poor at using logic, they are easily fooled into thinking "Well, if we need to have **some** savings to be able to invest in productive assets, then the **more** savings that we have available, the **more** we will invest in productive assets!" In other words, if a little savings is good, then a lot of savings must be better. Unfortunately for all of us, this is simply not true. In order to see why it is not true, consider the following thought experiment.

Imagine you have two buckets in front of you; one of which is labeled "**Save**" and the other is labeled "**Spend**". At your feet is a huge pile of $1.00 bills. Your job is to take each of the bills one at a time and put each one into one of the buckets.

Each time that you throw a dollar bill into the bucket labeled "Save" we can say that you just created a dollar of "savings". And each time that you throw a dollar bill into the bucket labeled "Spend" we can say that you just created a dollar of "demand". Therefore, you will be determining the nature of the economy through your choice of which bucket to throw the dollar bills into.

So, if you took all the dollar bills and threw them all into the "Spend" bucket, you would have created an economy that had tons of demand, but no savings available. In such an economy the unemployment rate would likely be quite low, but the economy would not grow much because it would be impossible for anyone to invest in the productive assets that the economy would need in order to grow.

On the other hand, if you took most of the dollars and threw them into the "Save" bucket, you would have created an economy that had tons of savings available, but not much demand. In such an economy there would be very little growth because there would be no incentive to invest any of the savings into productive assets. Without adequate demand, there is no incentive to increase production.

Therefore, it is important to recognize that the key to managing our economy is to strike a healthy balance between saving and spending. If we throw too many dollars into the "Spend" bucket, then we won't have the savings we need to be able to invest in productive assets. If we throw too many dollars into the "Save" bucket, the economy will lack the demand needed to support the investment in productive assets.

Unfortunately for all of us, the overwhelming size and complexity of our economy makes it impossible to determine the exact amount of savings we need. Instead, the best that we can do is to look for signs that we may have too much or too little and then adjust accordingly.

Currently there are many people who will ignorantly point to the high level of debt in our economy as "proof" that we do not save enough. It should be painfully obvious to you just how ridiculous this claim is.

After all, if I work hard and manage to save $10,000 this year and I put it into my savings account at the bank, *what is the bank going to do with that money*? Answer: they are going to move heaven and earth in an effort to lend it out to someone else. After all, banks do not make money by simply guarding our savings; they make money by lending our savings out to others and charging them interest on the loan.

So, the more savings we put in the bank, the more the bank is going to lend out. Thus, the more savings we have in our economy, the more debt we are going to have as well.

At this point some people might ignorantly claim that we should simply tell the banks to stop lending out so much money (because there is already too much debt in the economy). To see why this is such a bad idea, simply consider what would happen if we told the banks that they were not allowed to lend out any of our savings.

By telling the banks not to lend out our savings, you would effectively cut off one of their main sources of revenue. So, to make some money and be able to stay in business, the banks would naturally have to charge their customers a fee to guard their savings.

Obviously it does not make much sense for people to put their savings in the bank where it is going to lose value (due to the fees the bank is going to charge them). Therefore, many people would naturally opt to put their money in their mattress (or in a safe at home, or buried in the ground, etc.)

where it wouldn't cost them anything to store it. Once again, if I have to explain to you how sticking money in a mattress is not going to be good for the economy, then there truly is no hope for you.

(*One interesting side note*: In their infinite wisdom, the Federal Reserve Bank has decided to pay banks interest on the billions in excess savings the banks cannot lend out. In a free market, the banks would be forced to charge their customers for these excess savings. This would provide a disincentive to save, which would be good for the economy. So, by choosing to pay the banks for these excess savings, the Fed is doing the exact opposite of what the free market would do and harming the economy to boot!)

As it stands today, we have put so much savings into our banking system that the banks literally don't know what to do with it all. They have tried lending out as much as they possibly can, but they still have billions in excess reserves that they are not able to lend out. *Why won't the banks lend this money out?*

The banks won't lend this money out because they don't feel confident that the potential borrowers will have the income needed to pay back the loans; and the potential borrowers don't have the income because there is not enough demand in the economy (remember, one person's spending is another person's income); and there is not enough demand in our economy because we constantly throw too many dollars into the "Save" bucket.

Wait a minute! If it is so obvious that we have too much saving going on, then why do I constantly hear economists lamenting about the fact that Americans don't save enough?

Within a large segment of the economics community, there is a very strong desire to have economics thought of as being a "**hard science**". A hard science is one like chemistry or astronomy, where the scientists can use their knowledge to make accurate predictions about the future.

Now, for economics to be considered a hard science, it was necessary for economists to assume that people behave in much the same way that atoms or stars or planets behave. It was necessary for economists to assume that all economic participants are rational, intelligent beings whose behavior is logical and predictable.

Because of this assumption, economists have mistakenly developed the naïve theory that saving will always equal investment in productive assets. And since investment in productive assets is good for the economy, then it logically follows that saving is naturally good for the economy.

The traditional view of economics holds that as savings accumulates, the rate of return on these savings will naturally drop. As interest rates drop, people will naturally be incentivized to either consume more (since their saving is earning them so little) or to invest their savings into productive assets (to try and earn a higher rate of return). Either of these actions would help restore demand to the economy; thus, the market "corrects" itself due to the behavior of the rational market participants.

This view of the economy might be true in a world full of rational, well-educated people who know how to accurately read market signals. It is not true, however, in a world full of people who all fervently believe in the idiotic and irrational belief that "saving is good for the economy".

In such an economy, as savings accumulates, **people will just keep right on saving**. Even as demand weakens, debt soars and interest rates drop, people will inevitably fail to recognize that these are signals from the market that there is too much saving going on and they will continue to try and save even more.

The cycle goes like this: People save, which causes interest rates to drop, debt to increase and demand to fall. People look at the economy and think to themselves, "The economy is weak. Therefore, we need to do something that is good for the economy in order to get it back on track. Since saving is good for the economy, clearly we need to save more to turn the economy around!"

So, people will cram more savings into the financial system. This will in turn cause interest rates to fall even further, debt to increase and demand to remain weak. So, people will once again think to themselves, "The economy looks weak. Therefore, we need to do something that is good for the economy in order to get it back on track. Since saving is good for the economy, clearly we need to save more to turn the economy around!"

Thus, the ignorant belief that saving is good for the economy inevitably leads to a glut of savings and a dearth of demand. Without an adequate level of demand in the economy, it does not make financial sense to invest all our savings into productive assets. Therefore, a disproportionate amount of our savings inevitably gets invested into non-productive assets; primarily stocks.

(*Another interesting side note*: this process is further exacerbated by an insane tax code that treats the investment in non-productive assets more favorably than it does the investment in productive assets. Ahh, the infallible wisdom of our economic experts in Washington!)

Because there are so many people who mistakenly believe that stocks are productive assets, the rising stock market fools them into thinking that we are on the right track;

that we are growing richer as a nation. This in turn fools people into saving even more in order to invest in the rising stock market; which only serves to further weaken demand.

Of course, the only reason that people believe that a rising stock market represents an increase in real wealth is because they do not understand the nature of real wealth. They mistakenly believe that the value of our investments **equals** our wealth, when in reality the value of our investments merely **represents** our wealth. Our true wealth can only be measured by the value of our **production**.

Since we invest a disproportionate amount of our savings into non-productive assets, the value of these assets naturally rises faster than the value of the real wealth we can produce. As the difference between the value of our non-productive assets and the value of our production widens, people naturally begin to question how such high prices on our non-productive assets can be justified. So, economists and other financial *"experts"* are forced to come up with irrational, self-serving theories to justify the high asset prices.

Back in the late 1980s many *"experts"* believed that arbitrage and leveraged buyouts would allow us to unlock mysterious forms of "hidden wealth" from companies. In the 1990s the *"experts"* told us that the dot.coms were revolutionizing the very nature of business and thus would be able to generate untold amounts of wealth. And in the 2000s, the *"experts"* told us that higher housing prices were the result of sound economic fundamentals and thus could continue to support a dramatic increase in the amount of money being sunk into the mortgage market.

Because these theories never addressed the real reason why the asset prices were rising, cracks would eventually begin to appear in these façades. People would gradually begin to realize that the actual economy was much weaker than they originally believed and that the asset prices had risen much too far too soon. At some point a trigger would snap, bringing everyone back to reality and the stock market would come crashing down.

So, on the surface it would appear that the stock market crashes of the past several decades (1987, 2000, 2008) were all triggered by different crises, when in reality they were all caused by the same fundamental problem: our constant struggle to find a home for our excess savings.

Myth 7: Lower Rates will Spur the Economy

In an effort to spur the economy and get people back to work, the Federal Reserve Bank has been doing what it can to try and intentionally hold interest rates low in the naïve belief that this will spur additional demand for loans and inflate asset prices; both of which should help lead to an increase in spending, which should lead to new jobs being created.

Unfortunately, there are several major problems with this strategy. First of all, the **only way in which you can logically justify having the government intervene in the market in order to drive down interest rates is if you accept the proposition that the government knows better than the market where interest rates should be**. You would be extremely hard-pressed to convince me that such a proposition is even remotely close to being true.

Secondly, the Federal Reserve is run by economists. Thus, the Fed naturally operates under the misguided assumption that people are rational, intelligent beings. Because of this, the Fed mistakenly believes that lower interest rates will naturally lead to increased spending. However, as we saw in the previous chapter, because people ignorantly believe that saving is good for the economy, no matter how low interest rates go, people will simply continue to save.

Thirdly, the Fed also mistakenly believes that higher asset prices will make people **feel richer**, thus making them feel less compelled to save and more compelled to spend.

However, because people ignorantly believe that lower prices are good for the economy, that saving is good for the economy and that higher profits are good for the economy, they have essentially become "profit maximizers". Thus, no matter how rich they feel, they naturally want to do whatever they can to **make themselves even richer**. Thus, they will inevitably continue to save as much as they can regardless of how high the value of their assets climbs.

In fact, by "artificially" driving up asset prices, the Fed is more likely harming the economy than helping it. Because people are trying to **maximize** their wealth, they naturally do not want to miss out on any bull runs in the market. So, the rising asset prices **actually encourage people to save even more** in order to invest in the rising stock market. Of course, this only serves to further weaken the level of demand in the economy and to further inflate our non-productive asset values far above the value of our actual production; thus setting the stage for the next great market crash.

It is interesting to note that there are many people in this country who have been warning us that the Fed's policy of "easy money" and low interest rates will lead to sharp price increases and thus have been warning America that we are headed towards a state of hyperinflation where the prices on the general goods that we buy will spiral out of control. This would be true, except for one very important point.

We have already seen in the previous chapters how the wages paid to the working class are under tremendous pressure. These wages account for approximately 70% of the inflation as reported by the Consumer Price Index (CPI). So, without any wage growth, we are not likely to see any serious inflation (at least not as measured by the CPI). And we are not likely to see any real wage growth as long as people cling to the myths in this book.

The only way in which we would get any real inflation/wage growth would be if we experienced a truly remarkable increase in debt over a very short period of time. This will not occur simply from lower interest rates. It would take some other Black Swan event that required drastic action to justify the kind of debt levels we would need to overcome the economic force created by the beliefs in this book.

Lastly, and most importantly, the main flaw with the theory that lowering interest rates will help the economy may lie in the simple fact that it is highly unlikely that the government's actions are even having much of an effect on interest rates. While it is true that rates have generally declined over the past several decades (see the figure below), it is not at all clear that it was due to the government's actions.

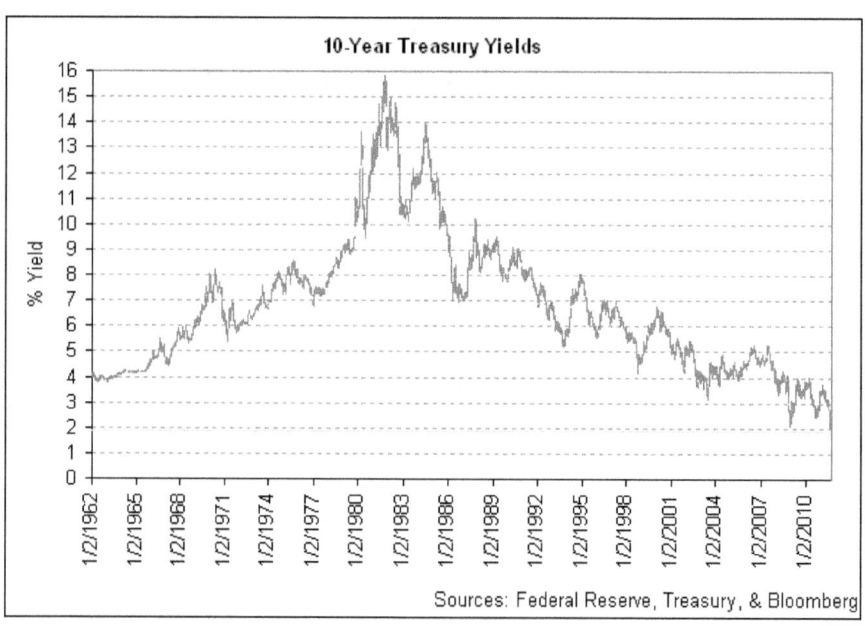

The real reason that rates have been declining for decades is quite simple. As we saw in the previous chapter, the problem with our economy for the past several decades has been the accumulation of an excessive amount of savings. So, as the amount of savings (i.e. capital) available in our economy has increased, the rate of interest that capital owners can charge for their capital has naturally declined; thus, the lower interest rates in our economy.

This combination of an excessive amount of capital and unsatisfactorily low returns on that capital has led to some rather interesting behavior in our financial system. First of all, it has made it possible for some investors to amass enough capital to take large equity positions in some very large companies.

Once they have established a large equity position in a company, these so-called "activist" investors can use their position as an owner of the company to demand changes to the company; changes that are designed to increase the return on their invested capital. This is typically done by increasing dividends or by increasing the amount of leverage being utilized by the company.

In some instances, these changes will also involve getting rid of the current CEO and/or Board Members. To do so, the activist investor simply needs to convince the other stockholders that the current management is to blame for the unsatisfactorily low returns on their capital.

The fascinating part of all this is the amount of pressure these fund managers can exert; not just on individual companies, but on the entire economy. To see why I say this, let us assume that there is a fund manager who has developed quite a reputation for "cleaning house" whenever he takes a stake in a company. Furthermore, let us assume he has enough capital under his management that he can buy a large equity stake in one of ten different companies.

Since none of the companies knows which one he is going to invest in, they are all essentially forced to take actions that they feel would preclude the manager from choosing their company. After all, the CEO and Board Members are fully aware of what a sweet gig their current job is, so they are naturally going to do whatever they can to keep it.

Therefore, the management of each company must do all it can to raise its returns to prevent the fund manager from taking a position in their company and demanding changes; changes that the current management is quite likely not to want to take. So even though the fund manager only has the **actual power** to shake up one company, the mere threat of his presence has the ability to change the behavior of all ten companies; **thus, his reach far exceeds his grasp**.

Many people have recognized the power these investors are able to exert and have mistakenly concluded that these investors must be stopped because they are harming the economy. What these people have failed to recognize is that these activist investors are simply taking our idiotic beliefs about our economy to their logical extreme.

As we saw in Myth 5, many people mistakenly believe that the main goal of a business is to increase its profitability. Thus, the activist investors aren't doing anything that is all that unique or untoward; they are merely adding fuel to the wrong fire. In other words, their actions are not the problem; their actions are merely a symptom of the problem. Their actions are a natural consequence of the idiotic beliefs that saving is good for the economy and that the main goal of any business is to maximize profitability.

The glut of capital that has arisen due to our excessive level of savings has naturally driven down the rate of return on interest bearing investments (bonds, mortgages, CDs, etc.). Thus, investors have naturally had to look for other ways to achieve higher returns. Some of them have figured out that they can achieve bigger returns by squeezing more profitability out of companies. In doing so, they are just doing what everyone else is doing; the only difference is that they are doing it on a bigger, and much more visible scale.

The glut of capital in our economy has also led to another interesting development. Since ordinary capital markets are often highly regulated, and consequently have somewhat limited returns, banks and other financial institutions have naturally sought out higher returns through the formation of the infamous "shadow banking system" (*a detailed discussion of which would take us far beyond the scope of this book*).

Unfortunately, by investing so much capital into unregulated markets that are often highly illiquid and generally not very well understood, the financial system has been put at great risk. We saw a glimpse of this risk in the most recent financial crisis.

Instead of addressing the core of the problem (the excess amount of savings in our system), many so-called *"experts"* have mistakenly pronounced that we need to regulate the shadow banking system in an effort to safeguard our economy from future crises; but this view is naïve.

If more excess savings keeps piling up, it is going to get harder and harder for people to earn a satisfactory return on those savings. Thus, they are going to be forced to take on more and more risk in order to earn the returns they are looking for. To do so they will simply look for ways around whatever new regulations our *"experts"* try to impose upon them.

By forcing more risk in the system, without addressing the real problem, we are only setting the system up for an epic fail; we are simply "priming the pump" for another financial collapse.

Myth 8: A Smaller Government will be Good

As I mentioned in our discussion of Myth 5, every company in the world should be focused on becoming more productive. Similarly, our leaders in Washington need to focus on making our government more productive. Doing so will likely make the government smaller, but it is critical for us as a nation to recognize that **simply making our government smaller will not necessarily make it more productive**.

For example, let us assume that we just blindly cut the amount of money that the government spends on repairing our roads and bridges. This would instantly make the government smaller (since it is now spending less than it did before), but it would not make it more productive.

The decreased level of road maintenance would inevitably lead to more cracks and potholes in our roads. Driving over this rough surface would result in increased wear on our tires, so we end up having to replace them sooner. If the potholes become bad enough, hitting them will cause our cars to go out of alignment. Even minor changes in your car's alignment can reduce the gas mileage your car gets; major alignment problems will entail repair expenses; so, we wind up spending more on gas and repairs.

If the potholes worsen still, they will cause accidents. So, we will incur repair bills on our cars and medical expenses for the injured. In addition, those of us stuck in the traffic jams that result from the accident will waste gas and our economy will suffer from a decline in productivity.

So, even though we "saved" money in the short run by reducing the amount of money the government spent on roads, we ended up just spending that money on gas, repairs and medical bills. Even worse, the resulting decline in productivity caused by the injuries, the traffic jams and people waiting to get their car repaired, **will actually cause the economy to shrink**. The point being that any reduction in government spending is going to need to be carefully thought out to assure us that the reductions will not cause more harm than good.

Unfortunately for all of us, it seems as though there are many people in this country that just don't understand this. In fact, if you listen to some economic "*experts*", one cannot help but think that every single dollar the government spends is a drag on the economy and every single dollar spent by the private sector is a boon to the economy. It should be obvious to you that this just isn't so. After all, when we measure the size of "the economy", we basically just add up all the money that is spent during the year.

In order to help us get a clearer picture of what is going on in the economy, our total level of spending is often broken down into two sectors: private sector spending (the spending done by consumers and businesses) and public sector spending (the spending done by the government).

To see how this works, let us assume there is an island economy with 1,000 people. The average income on the island is $1,000 and there is currently no saving done on the island. Therefore, we can say that annual demand equals $1,000,000 (= 1,000 * $1,000). In this example, we would say that private sector spending is equal to $1,000,000 per year and public sector spending is equal to $0 per year; because there currently is no government on the island.

Now let us say that the islanders all decide that they need a government to help settle disputes, build some roads, enforce laws, etc. So, they elect a chief to run this new organization and they all agree to give the chief 20% of their income every year in order to fund the government.

Therefore, the average amount of money available to be spent by each resident would be reduced by the 20% they give to the government. In other words, we could say that the average after tax income on the island would be $800 (= $1,000 − ($1,000 * 20%)). Thus, we can now see that private sector spending on the island has fallen to $800,000 per year (= 1,000 * $800).

On the other hand, we can also see that public sector spending has risen to $200,000 (= 1,000 * $200). So in total, "the economy" is still equal to $1,000,000 (= $800,000 + $200,000). Thus, we can see that increasing taxes and government spending did not shrink the economy; it merely changed who did the spending and what the spending was for.

Now let us further assume that a crazy witch doctor visits the island and starts ranting and raving about how "saving is good for the economy". He is so passionate and seems so certain that everyone on the island decides to save 10% of their income. Thus, the amount of money spent by the average islander drops to $700 (= $800 − ($1,000 * 10%)). Thus, we can now see that private sector spending in the island economy has fallen to $700,000 (= 1,000 * $700).

Not surprisingly, many of the residents begin to complain that business seems to be lackluster; that demand seems to be weaker than before. In addition, some of them begin to suggest that the newly formed government might be the source of the problem. The chief hears of this and decides that he must quickly do something that will lift the level of demand in the economy.

After consulting the crazy witch doctor, the chief decides to borrow the $100,000 that the islanders saved and use the proceeds to "stimulate the economy". So, the chief issues bonds that the residents then purchase with their savings. In return, the chief promises to pay the islanders interest on the bonds and he promises that he will restore overall demand in the economy.

The chief spends the $100,000 in bond proceeds on some new roads and thus overall demand in the economy has been restored to $1,000,000 (The private sector spending of $700,000 plus the original public sector spending of $200,000 plus the stimulus spending of $100,000).

Unfortunately for the island economy, the next year the islanders once again save 10% of their income. So now the chief is faced with an even more serious problem. With private sector spending stuck at $700,000 per year, the chief has to come up with $300,000 in public sector spending just to keep the economy from shrinking. He only has the $200,000 in tax revenue at his disposal, so he is forced to once again borrow another $100,000 to spend on yet another stimulus program.

Not only that, but the chief also must come up with a way to pay the interest on what he has already borrowed. Since he cannot cut spending without lowering demand, he must also **borrow even more money** to make the interest payments. Assuming that this cycle continues for several years, it is easy to see that the island government is going to be drowning in debt rather quickly.

This little example highlights the dilemma currently faced by our government. As we have seen, our economy is suffering from a fundamental lack of demand due to our excessive level of savings. Because neither political party seems to understand this, **both Republicans and Democrats alike** have been trying to utilize significant deficit spending programs in order to try and inject some demand into the economy. Unfortunately for all of us, these deficit spending programs have done nothing to improve our economy because they do not address the fundamental problem with our economy.

If the idea of using deficit spending to stimulate the economy is so obviously flawed, why on earth did we ever decide to use it in the first place?

Because some of the crazy witch doctors in our economy ignorantly believe that it will work, and the public is too poorly educated to see why it won't work.

Here is the basic theory on deficit spending: The government borrows money and spends it; thus, raising the level of demand in the economy (which is true). Businesses see the level of demand pick up and thus immediately invest in the economy to satisfy this new demand (which is **NOT** true). This investment creates more demand, which encourages businesses to invest even more into the economy and suddenly the economy is growing like gangbusters (this would be true if the second part were true)!

So why is the second part NOT true? After all, it sounds pretty reasonable.

Unfortunately, there are several major flaws with this theory. First of all, businesses realize that deficit spending is only providing a temporary lift to the economy. They can see that our mounting debt appears to be getting out of hand and they know that at some point the government is going to have to cut its spending. When it does, demand will fall. Therefore, businesses do not want to fully invest in the economy when they know that our current level of demand is only temporary.

In addition, by constantly utilizing these stimulus programs, the government is constantly reinforcing the idea that there is something "wrong" with the economy. This in turn breeds a lack of confidence in both individuals and businesses alike. This lack of confidence then leads to a hesitancy to fully invest in an economy that is obviously weak. Thus, the stimulus programs do more to weaken the economy; not help it.

Even more importantly, as we saw in Myth 5, businesses have been ignorantly told to maximize their own value. So, if they see a pickup in demand, the first thing they do is **absolutely nothing**. That is, they will wait and see if their current workforce can handle the additional demand. After all, **hiring people costs money**; which lowers profits and the value of the firm. If the increased demand can be handled with the current level of expenses, profits will go up; as will the value of the firm.

If the current workforce simply cannot handle the increase in demand, the business will next look to make a minimal investment to help the current workforce. The businesses will upgrade their tools and processes, but only to the extent that is needed to satisfy the increase in demand; but no more than that.

Lastly, if that modest investment is still not enough, then as a last resort, businesses will look to invest in more productive assets and hire more workers. So, the things that we need to truly turn the economy around, is the **last option** that business will choose when faced with rising demand.

So, the stimulus programs do help to restore (at least temporarily) some of the demand that is lost due to our savings, and even help to raise the profitability of the businesses in our economy. However, the programs do not help to generate the full-scale investment needed to truly turn our economy around, mainly because so many people have been trained to believe in the idiotic myths outlined in this book.

Thus, the government is continually forced to borrow more and more to prop up our flagging demand. The idea that this cycle can be broken by **reducing** the level of government spending is absolutely absurd.

After all, the only reason you have a job (if you are fortunate enough to have a job) is because other people **spend money**. They either buy a good or service directly from you, or from the company that you work for. So, thinking that it will be "good" for the economy if we do the exact opposite of the one thing that keeps you employed is ridiculous.

Now, there are some people who recognize that drastic spending cuts will severely hurt the economy, but many of these people have mistakenly jumped to the conclusion that we should continue with our massive deficit spending to grow the economy. I guess in some ways this type of thinking is only natural, but it is just as flawed as the idea that we should start hacking away at government spending.

To see why I say this, let us assume that a man has eaten nothing but junk food for the past ten years. He goes to the doctor. The doctor tells him that his poor diet has caused him to become dangerously overweight and has led to diabetes and heart disease. So, the man decides that for the next year he won't eat anything at all.

The point of this story is that just because you have been doing the "wrong" thing for a long time, it doesn't automatically follow that doing the exact opposite will be the "right" thing. The government has been spending too much, but immediately stopping spending is not the answer; and continuing with our massive deficit is not the answer.

So, what is the answer?

Once again, we need to step back for a moment and recognize that the economy isn't struggling because of technical issues (debt, prices, taxes, etc.); the economy is struggling because of an ignorant belief system. Due to a serious deficiency of meaningful economic education in our educational system, the public is constantly being misled into believing ideas about the economy that just aren't true.

In order to prevent yet another financial crisis brought about by a system clogged with excess savings, we need to understand what truly grows an economy, so we can focus our attention on the things that can truly improve our situation. So "the answer" to our debt dilemma is that we need to change people's beliefs. In the next chapter we will take a big step forward in the process of changing our beliefs by looking at a very simple example that highlights how an economy actually grows.

Myth 9: Wealth creates Jobs

It is easy to see why so many people believe in this myth. After all, if a wealthy person hires some workers to fix up his house, clearly he has created some jobs. But simply saying that it was the "wealth" that created the jobs is naïve.

In order to more fully understand the nature of job creation you need to be able to recognize that **the creation of wealth** creates the **opportunity** for job creation, but it does not guarantee that jobs will actually be created.

To illustrate what I mean by this, let us look at the following analogy (which is loosely based upon Peter Schiff's island analogy). Suppose we have an island nation where the inhabitants are all naked and homeless. They spend all their time trying to catch fish with their bare hands just to stay alive.

One day, one of the islanders (let us call him Pat) fashions a net out of some sticks and palm fronds. With this net it only takes Pat about an hour to catch a fish.

The island Chief is so amazed with Pat's invention that she quickly becomes quite concerned with the power that the net provides to its user. The Chief worries that if all the islanders can get fish so easily, they may decide that they don't need her anymore. So, fearing that the islanders will overthrow her if they all obtain such a powerful tool, the Chief immediately passes a law forbidding anyone else from making another net.

Initially, Pat just uses the net to catch one fish first thing in the morning and then he spends the rest of the day just goofing around; so life on the island really doesn't change very much.

Eventually Pat realizes that instead of just goofing around, he could spend his time catching several fish and then use his extra fish to pay others to do some tasks that he would like done; like build a house to keep him dry and make some fashionable clothes for him to wear. Therefore, he hires other people to do these jobs for him and pays them in fish so they don't have to spend all day catching one on their own.

Let us assume that this goes on for several years; by now Pat has a gigantic house and lots of snazzy clothes to wear. Not surprisingly, the other islanders start to get tired of Pat's opulence, so they complain to the Chief that it isn't fair that Pat gets to live in a huge house and wear fancy clothes while they have nothing. In an effort to keep the peace, the Chief tries to get Pat to share some of his wealth, but Pat adamantly refuses.

Eventually the islanders become so frustrated with the situation that they overthrow the Chief and set up a new law that says Pat must share his wealth. Pat is furious with this new development, so he packs up all his belongings and leaves the island.

Now, at first blush this may seem like a disaster for the island. After all, all the wealth is gone! But in reality, it is the best thing that could have happened to them. With Pat and the Chief out of the picture, the remaining islanders are now free to build their own nets. Soon the islanders can catch many fish and the island economy quickly flourishes.

There are several things that you need to recognize about this story. First of all, through the introduction of an effective, timesaving technology (the net), **wealth was created**.

That is, the islanders were able to produce more goods of value (fish) than they could before.

Secondly, jobs were only created when Pat decided to **spend** some of the wealth created by the net. When he was being lazy and just goofing around all day, Pat was essentially **hoarding the productive capacity of the net for himself**. In doing so, he prevented the island economy from growing and prevented the creation of any jobs. It was only when he **utilized the productive capacity of the net,** and **spent the wealth generated by the net,** that jobs were able to be created.

Thirdly, because he refused to share the increased amount of wealth now available to the island, Pat himself became quite rich. Had he been feeling a little more egalitarian, Pat could have easily chosen to share some of his extra fish; thus, raising everyone's standard of living. Of course, this would have also meant that none of them would have been rich because they all would have experienced the same increase.

Lastly, **and most importantly**, it is critical to recognize that **getting rid of Pat and the Chief was better for the island as a whole than just making Pat share what he had**. If Pat had simply agreed to share his fishes, then there would still be only one net on the island; which would mean **that the productivity of the island would still be quite limited.**

By not allowing the other islanders to build their own nets, the Chief limited how much the economy could grow because she **limited how productive the other island members could become**. Once all the islanders had access to a net, they **all** became much more productive and thus the island economy truly prospered.

In today's world it is currently quite fashionable among some economists to claim that our economy is being held back by excessive government regulations. Unfortunately for all of us, these economists have a very weak understanding of economic activity. They mistakenly think that it is the wealth that drives the economy, when in fact it is **productivity that drives wealth**.

Because they fail to understand this, these economists naively propose that we should remove regulations that merely hurt the **profitability** of corporations; not their **productivity**. But as we already saw with Myth 5, focusing on profitability has done nothing to improve the well-being of the working class or of the economy in general.

So, instead of naively focusing on corporate profitability, what we really need to focus on are any issues that hinder **productivity**. And in a rather ironic twist, it is the corporations that are the guiltiest here; not the government.

Whenever a company here in the US develops a new productivity improvement (be it a new drug, a new technology or a timesaving process), *do they freely share it with everyone else*? Of course not. They fight like hell to keep it to themselves using patents, confidentiality agreements, etc.

By not freely disseminating productivity improvements throughout our entire economy, corporations are guilty of limiting the amount of economic growth we could achieve; just as the Chief limited the growth of the island economy by not allowing everyone to have their own net.

Of course, it is easy to see that corporations prevent the dissemination of productivity improvements primarily because of a couple of the myths in this book. By mistakenly viewing life as being a competition, corporations are naturally resistant to sharing productivity improvements with their competition because they want to hang onto every advantage that they can get.

Additionally, by mistakenly thinking that the main goal of a business is to maximize profits, corporations naturally try and protect their innovations to try and make themselves more profitable than other companies. Thus, they naturally try and keep things of economic value away from other companies.

To make matters worse, not only are corporations hoarding productive capacity for themselves through their use of patents, but they are also hoarding cash (wealth) as well. As I alluded to earlier, US corporations have somewhere close to $2 trillion in cash on their balance sheets. To put this in terms of our island analogy, imagine if Pat used his net to catch several fish each day, but then did nothing with them; he just built a big stockpile of fish for himself. This is essentially what many corporations are doing here in the US.

Instead of investing all the wealth they generate back into the economy, corporations are currently storing much of that wealth in the form of cash on their balance sheets. It is easy to see that there are two rather obvious factors driving this behavior.

First of all, their hoarding of their cash actually does make the economy weaker, thus making any investment into productive assets much less attractive from a financial standpoint. Secondly, they have figured out that hoarding the cash helps to drive up their own stock price; which the executive's compensation is often tied directly to.

Again, we need to be able to recognize that this behavior is all related back to the myth that the main goal of the business is to maximize profits; when businesses really should be focused on increasing productivity. So, in order to get corporations to invest the massive amount of wealth at their disposal, we will first need to refocus their goals.

Returning to our focus on job creation, we also need to be able to recognize that there is a big difference between wealth **creation** and wealth **accumulation**. To see what I mean by this, let us return to our island analogy.

Let us assume that shortly after Pat develops his net, along comes another islander named Brutus. Brutus is the biggest and meanest person on the island. He is also quite clever and quickly realizes that the net can generate quite a bit of wealth, so Brutus goes to Pat and offers him a deal. Brutus will agree to protect Pat from "accidents" if Pat gives him six fish per day. Since he is terrified of Brutus, Pat reluctantly agrees. Under this new arrangement, Brutus quickly becomes quite wealthy.

In this scenario it is easy to see that even though Brutus became quite wealthy, he did not **create** any wealth; he simply accumulated the wealth created by Pat. Similarly, not everyone in our world who becomes wealthy does so by creating wealth. Some people become wealthy simply by accumulating wealth from others.

For example, let us assume that there is a successful pillow factory that pays its workers $10 an hour and sells its pillows for $20. Let us further assume that a woman named Lisa decides to open a new pillow factory. Lisa sets up her factory to be just like the other factory, so that Lisa's factory produces the same number of pillows per hour and of the same quality.

The key difference being that Lisa recognizes there are many unemployed people in the area that would be willing to work in her factory for only $9 an hour. Due to the lower wages she pays her workers, Lisa can sell her pillows for less than the $20 that the other company charges. Let us assume that she sells the pillows for $18 and that over time Lisa's company becomes quite successful and the first pillow factory goes out of business.

In this instance, it is critical for you to be able to recognize that Lisa did not **create** any wealth or any jobs (even though she is now wealthy and employs many people) because she did not introduce any productivity improvements into the economy. She simply accumulated wealth that already existed.

You might say, "But *what about the customers? Aren't they better off since they can now get a pillow for less money?*" Yes, they are, but their gains came entirely at the expense of the workers. Since Lisa did not introduce any productivity improvements into the economy, the economy did not grow. Instead, Lisa merely captured the wealth that already existed by getting her workers to work for less than the workers in the original factory.

Had Lisa devised a new technology or production system that allowed her factory to make pillows more efficiently, she could have left the workers' wages at $10 per hour and still sold her pillows for less than the other factory. In this case Lisa would have created wealth and the economy would have truly grown.

In our discussion of Myth 1, I had alluded to a couple of facts regarding the efforts of poor people trying to get some wealth for themselves. I had mentioned that creating wealth was not nearly as easy as many people seem to think and that the economic beliefs we have chosen to believe in make it exceedingly unlikely that any new wealth generated by our economy will find its way to the poor.

We have already seen in Myth 4 how our irrational belief that lower prices are good for the economy is putting a tremendous amount of downward pressure on the wages of the working class; thus preventing wealth from reaching the working class.

Additionally, as we just saw with our story about Lisa and the pillow factory, to truly **create** wealth, you must be **more productive** than the current businesses in the economy or you simply wind up taking wealth away from somebody else.

So, for any individual to **truly create new wealth**, they cannot simply start up a business. They must start a business that is more productive than the other businesses in the economy that currently provide the same good or service. Or they must start up a business that produces a good or service that is entirely unique; that nobody else is producing. Either of these options would represent an extremely difficult challenge to anyone in this country; even more so for a poor person with few resources at his or her disposal.

Before we move on to the next chapter, there is another important issue that we need to address. In order for a good or service to be consumed, it first has to be produced. So, our ability to consume, and therefore the size of our economy, is going to be constrained by our level of productivity. In short, the more productive we can become, the more we can produce. The more we can produce, the more we can consume. The more we consume, the larger our economy.

Obviously, our desire for consumption has a direct bearing on our incentive to produce. After all, if you do not believe anybody is going to consume your goods/services, then there is no incentive for you to produce any goods/services.

This brings up two interesting points. First of all, it sort of leads us to a "chicken or the egg" type dilemma. Which one really leads to economic growth, the production of goods and services or the desire to consume goods and services?

Without the desire to consume, there is no incentive to produce. But without production, there is no income. Without income, there can be no consumption; no matter how much desire for consumption there may be.

Secondly, it should be clear that by repeatedly telling people that they need to save more (i.e. consume less), we are lowering the desire for consumption. Thus, we are lowering the incentive to produce which makes businesses more hesitant to invest in their productive capability.

Myth 10: Free Trade is Good/Bad

To help us understand how trade can be so important and valuable to our economy, let us consider the following lesson. Imagine we have an island nation with 10 inhabitants. Initially they all go about doing their own thing. That is, each person provides their own shelter, grows their own food, makes their own clothes, etc.

Eventually they figure out that they will be much more productive if each of them focuses on a specific task, instead of having each of them try to do everything for themselves. As we discussed in Myth 4, specialization of tasks leads to higher productivity, and it is productivity that determines how much wealth we can produce.

So, one person on the island is assigned the task of making clothes, one person is assigned the task of growing food, one person builds shelters, etc. They then trade with each other so that everybody gets what they need. In this way they will all be better off because they will be able to produce much more value than they could when they were trying to do everything on their own.

Even if we then took each person and placed them on their own island and let them form their own country, it would still be in their best interests for them to continue focusing on specific tasks and trading with one another for the other goods/services they need. Thus, **in an ideal world**, "Free

Trade" is always good for the economy because it allows for people to become as productive as possible.

As I mentioned earlier, economists tend to believe that human beings are rational, intelligent beings. Thus, many of them naturally assume that since Free Trade is good in an ideal world, we should naturally try and pursue Free Trade in our own world. Because they mistakenly believe that people are rational and intelligent, they naturally assume that people will always utilize trade "**for the right reasons**" and that trade will inevitably lead to a stronger economy.

However, as we have also seen, people are clearly **NOT** rational, intelligent beings. Instead, they are irrational, poorly educated creatures who generally labor under the misguided beliefs that "Life is a Competition", that "Low Prices are Good for America", that the "Main Goal of a Business is to Maximize Profits", etc. Because people operate under these misguided beliefs, they do not use trade as it is intended (i.e. they do not use trade to raise their **productivity**), instead they use trade to try and raise their **profitability**.

Consumers use trade as simply another tool with which to pursue their naïve quest for lower prices. Businesses don't use trade to raise their productivity, they use it to lower their costs. Thus, trade in the real world does not always make the economy stronger; instead it merely adds fuel to the fire created by the myths outlined in this book.

To complicate matters even further, because people in different countries tend to hold fundamentally different beliefs about the world we live in, they naturally develop very different views on how the world should work. That is, they develop very different views on the role of government; how to implement taxes; how to pursue monetary policies; what items hold the most economic value; etc. Thus, in the real world there are significant differences in the rules and regulations that each nation establishes regarding economic activity.

To help us understand how this leads to problems in the global economy, imagine if the NFL decided to allow each team to tweak the rules of the game as they saw fit. So, one team might decide that the offense should have more people on the field than the defense; another team might decide that it is legal for offensive lineman to grab and hold onto defensive lineman; another team may decide that several offensive players can be in motion at the same time; and so on.

As one might imagine, the games would quickly become quite chaotic. Even more importantly, since each team was playing by a different set of rules, there would be no way for the referees to determine who was cheating and who was not.

The same is basically true of our economy. Because each country has essentially been allowed to tweak the "rules" of economic activity as they see fit, there is really no way to determine who is cheating and who is not since each country is playing by its own rules.

So, to summarize our situation, we have a world full of irrational idiots who ignorantly cling to the myths outlined in this book. Therefore, we are naturally faced with a myriad of economic problems (i.e. trade deficits, widening wealth gap, rising long-term unemployment, weak growth, etc.).

Because human beings have an unerring tendency to believe in ideas that are ideally suited to their own personal experience, each nation naturally becomes convinced that they are the "good guy" (because they follow their own rules) and that everyone else is the "bad guy" (because they play by a different set of rules). So instead of recognizing that the real cause of our problems is our idiotic belief structure, everybody basically stands around blaming each other for all the obvious "cheating" that is going on.

The most unfortunate side effect of this situation is that many people in our economy have begun to adopt the ignorant belief **that all trade is bad**. Setting the stage for one of the most laughably ignorant debates of all time. On one side you have the idiot economists insisting that trade is always a good thing (which it would be in an ideal world, which we do not live in) and the idiot anti-trade people who ignorantly claim that trade is the "cause" of all the harm we see in our economy (even though trade is the basis of all economic activity).

In the short run, to prevent more people from adopting an "anti-trade" point of view, it will probably be in everyone's interest to moderate trade a little bit. This will allow us to achieve greater political stability; which will become a priceless commodity in the coming decades.

In the long run, however, we desperately need to improve our educational system. We need to educate people about the myths outlined in this book and the harm they are doing to our economy. We also need to teach people about the important role that trade can play in our economy and the importance of creating a universal economic framework that will allow each country to play by the same rules.

Myth 11: Market Efficiency

The formal idea of market efficiency was developed sometime around 1970 by economist Eugene Fama. His theory (the Efficient Market Hypothesis) basically stated that it is not possible for an investor to regularly outperform the market because all available information is already built into stock prices.

This is one of those ideas that is so ridiculous it is difficult to comprehend how so many people could believe it to be true. It is yet another powerful testimony as to how effective our thought process is at fooling people into thinking that they understand how the world really works, even when they are complete idiots.

In order to better understand what is wrong with this idea, we really need to split the idea into two components:

1. All available information is already built into stock prices

2. It is not possible for an investor to outperform the market

There are so many things wrong with the first component that it is difficult to know where to even start. First of all, there is simply too much information generated by our global economy for it to ALL be built into stock prices. After all, our global economy is comprised of roughly 8 billion people who are all scattered amongst hundreds of different countries and literally millions of different municipalities. And each of these areas is subject to its own rules, regulations, culture, etc.

There are literally trillions and trillions of economic transactions occurring each day and each one of these transactions helps to shape our economy. If you think that there is any way for the market to accurately assess this mind-boggling array of information, then there is something seriously wrong with you. Additionally, even if we could somehow capture all that information, there would be no possible way for us to process it all.

A second problem comes from the simple fact that there will always be a great deal of data asymmetry in our world. There is no escaping the fact that some people will have much more time available to devote to collecting and analyzing economic data. If you already work a full-time job and are trying to raise a family, there is no way in hell you will be able to assess as much data as a professional stock picker.

The third problem with the first component is that there seems to be an implied assumption in it that all information is always incorporated "properly" into stock prices. It seems to imply that people never make mistakes in processing the information that is available. But this isn't even remotely true.

People constantly make mistakes due to a lack of proper training, a general lack of intelligence, being blinded by personal emotions, the effects of the asymmetry of information, being deceived by the myths in this book and many other reasons.

While these three issues are certainly problematic for incorporating information into stock prices, there is one more issue to look at that is much more important than the first three combined. And that is the fact that ALL of the information in our economy is deeply, deeply flawed in one critical respect.

To see why I say this, you need to first recognize that there are many different models and techniques that can be used when trying to calculate what the stock price for a company should be. But no matter which method is used, it should be clear to you that they will all be influenced by the monies flowing into and out of the corporation.

Obviously, the monies flowing into the corporation are determined by the amount of goods/services the company sells at a certain price. And of course, the monies flowing out of the corporation are determined by the amount of goods/services the company purchases at a certain price. Thus, before we can even begin to understand if all information is accurately reflected into a stock price, we first need to understand the nature of the prices of all the goods/services in the economy, since they determine the amount of money flowing into and out of corporations.

Because of the flaws in our educational system, many people mistakenly believe that the actual purchase/sale price for any good or service in our economy is the "true" price for that good or service; that is not correct. Instead, we need to recognize that the "true" price for any good or service is what we might call the **True Economic Value (TEV) of that good or service**.

This TEV represents the price at which we achieve optimal economic activity. It is the price at which people make the most effective economic decisions. If we deviate too far from the TEV, then people will make poor decisions and the economy will suffer.

If a magical fairy came to earth and convinced everyone that the price of a barrel oil should be permanently set at $5 a barrel, it would lead to bad decisions. Producers of oil would not be able to bring in enough revenue to stay in business. Thus, nobody would get any oil at all.

Similarly, if the fairy permanently changed the price of oil to $500 a barrel, producers would be incentivized to produce too much, while consumers wouldn't be able to buy it at such a high price. So once again, producers go out of business and we wouldn't have any oil at all.

The point being that if prices are "wrong" (in either direction) it will lead people to make "wrong" decisions and the economy will suffer. The problem is that our economy is so large and complicated there is no way for us to truly know what the TEV is for any of the goods and services that we consume.

For example, let us say that a sandwich shop sells a Turkey Sub for $6.99; thus $6.99 is the **actual price**. The TEV of that sandwich, however, will be different from the $6.99. To see why I say this, let us consider the turkey sub from the perspective of only three different people.

First there is Joe who absolutely loves turkey subs. Second there is Sam who is a vegetarian. Lastly there is Harry who much prefers burgers to turkey subs. It shouldn't take a rocket scientist to figure out that each of these individuals is going to value the turkey sub differently.

To further complicate matters, not only does each individual have a different TEV for the turkey sub, but the TEV for each person will vary wildly throughout the course of a day. If we find that Joe hasn't eaten all day, we would find his TEV to be much higher than it would be if he just finished off a huge plate of spaghetti. His TEV at noon will be much different from his TEV at 2:00am.

In addition, the TEV for all the ingredients in the turkey sub cannot be specifically determined either. The TEV of the turkey alone is influenced by thousands of different factors. The reproduction rate of the turkeys, transportation costs, insurance rates, diseases, new farm formation, trade tariffs, labor costs, feed costs, weather patterns, consumer demographics, increases/decreases in other meat supplies, etc. Of course, all the other ingredients that go into the sub are all subject to the same types of influences.

Because it is impossible for businesses to take all this into account, they are essentially forced to take a crude guess at what the most effective actual price will be for goods and services they purchase and sell. But one thing is absolutely certain, **the actual price of ANY good or service will never perfectly reflect the TEV of that good or service because the TEV is much too volatile and ephemeral to ever be accurately measured**.

Therefore, all the monies that flow into and out of any given corporation are based on prices that are "wrong", in that they are all based on prices that do not reflect the TEV for the goods and services being produced or consumed by the corporation. I shouldn't have to say this, but, if the price of every single good and service coming into or going out of a corporation is "wrong", there is no way in hell we are going to be able to calculate a stock price for that corporation that isn't "wrong" as well.

So, if every single price in the world is "wrong", then what effect does this "wrongness" have on our economy?

Since people are always making decisions based upon "wrong" prices, they naturally make "wrong" decisions. The good news is that this generally does not prove to be much of an issue because the number of people who wrongly believe that the price of an entity is "too high" is commonly offset by a similar number of people who wrongly believe that the price is "too low". So, the two sides basically cancel each other out.

Occasionally, however, an overwhelming number of people will all make a series of decisions in one direction or the other; causing the price of some entity to become unusually high or low. Fortunately for us, the basic laws of supply and demand normally kick in and prevent the prices from becoming way out of line, thus preventing any major damage to our economy.

Because each of us has a limited amount of wealth at our disposal, we are forced to make choices as to what we spend that wealth on. We cannot afford to buy "everything" that we might want, so we must decide how badly we want each item on our wish list.

So, as the price of a specific item goes up, demand for that item will generally fall because many people will naturally decide that the item will take up too much of their wealth and will decide to buy something else on their wish list instead.

The reverse is also true. If the price of a specific item falls, then demand for that item will generally pick up, thus raising the price. Thus, prices tend to not get "too high" or "too low".

However, over time, certain myths develop within the economy that cause people to ignore the basic laws of supply and demand. These myths basically cloud people's judgment; thus, leading to prices that are **significantly** out of line with reality.

The myths that we have been discussing in this book are just one type of myth that can cloud people's judgement. We can call the myths outlined in this book "overarching myths" because they are not restricted to a specific period of time. They have already been around for a long time and will unfortunately probably be around for quite some time to come.

These "overarching myths" basically set the stage for an economic crisis. They lay the groundwork for what are commonly called "bubbles" in our economy. These bubbles are simply cases of extreme mispricing; where the price of an economic entity (or entities) become(s) ridiculously high. They are an inevitable result of an excess of capital in our economy that is always chasing too little demand.

Eventually the overarching myths in this book combine forces with what we might call a "period specific myth" and a significant bubble is born. For instance, back in the 1980s it became quite fashionable to believe that our newfound use of derivatives and leverage were going to allow businesses to unlock a tremendous amount of wealth from our economy. This **period specific myth** then combined with the **overarching myths** outlined in this book to create the stock market bubble (and subsequent crash) in the late 1980s.

Then, in the 1990s it became quite popular to believe that the "dot.coms" were fundamentally changing the business world as we know it and would allow the economy to achieve extraordinary growth. This period specific myth combined with the myths in this book to create the stock market bubble (and subsequent crash) in the early 2000s.

Then, in the early 2000s it became quite popular to believe that our rising housing prices were the result of strong economic fundamentals and the effects of the supposed "Great Moderation". This period specific myth then combined with the myths in this book to create the Financial Crisis of 2008.

Proponents of the Efficient Market Hypothesis have an extremely difficult time trying to explain why the stock market keeps developing bubbles and crashing. After all, if all relevant information is reflected in stock market prices, then *how on earth can stock market prices be so inaccurate? How can they drop so much in such a short period of time?*

By recognizing that **all prices are always "wrong"**, it becomes easy to see why bubbles and crashes occur on a regular basis. People tend not to recognize bubbles until it is too late because prices were "wrong" even before the bubble developed; prices were also "wrong" as the bubble formed; and prices were still "wrong" after the bubble burst. Thus, we cannot recognize when prices are "wrong" **because prices are always "wrong"**.

Somewhat ironically, the misguided concept of market efficiency helps these bubbles become even larger than they otherwise might. By training people to believe in the foolish notion that all information is reflected in stock prices, people naturally tend to believe that the stock market is in some sense "correct". Thus, people are not as concerned about the formation of bubbles as they otherwise might be. So, they are more likely to "let their guard down" and are more easily fooled into following the latest periodic myths.

Returning to our original discussion, we can easily see that the first part of the theory (that all information is reflected in stock prices) is clearly not true. However, it is still possible to save the second part of the theory (the idea that an investor cannot beat the market). To do so we simply need to recognize the effect of what we have already discussed; that people are irrational idiots and that prices are always wrong.

In such an environment there will be no systematic way to beat the market for two simple reasons. Firstly, if all prices in our economy are always wrong, then no matter how much analysis you do, you are still just analyzing mispriced data; your analysis will never be "true".

Secondly, even if by some miracle you developed a "correct" stock price for a company like IBM, you still would not be able to develop a sure-fire method to take advantage of this information because there is no telling what decisions an irrational idiot is going to make. There is no guarantee that you will be able to make money with a "correct" price of IBM because people (and thus the market) can stay irrational far longer than you can remain solvent.

For example, let us assume that you could travel back in time several hundred years and place a bet with the people in the past that the earth is round. Even though you were "correct", you still would have lost money on your bet for centuries. Thus, you would have gone bankrupt long before the "correctness" of your bet was ever realized.

Myth 12: Data is King

As I mentioned earlier in this book, within a large segment of the economics community, there is a very strong desire to have economics thought of as being a hard science. And for economics to be considered a hard science, it was necessary for economists to assume that all economic participants are rational, intelligent beings.

In addition, for economics to be considered a hard science it was also necessary for economists to assume that data analysis could be performed on our economy in much the same way that a chemist can conduct analysis on the behavior of elements, molecules, etc. Or in much the same way that an astronomer conducts analysis on the motion of planets and galaxies.

Economists naturally assumed that their analysis would subsequently yield important economic truths which could then be used to help predict our economic future. That the analysis could create the insight we need to understand what economic policies we should implement to overcome any economic difficulties we might be facing.

Unfortunately for all of us, just as the assumption that people are rational, intelligent creatures turned out to be incredibly naïve, so too has the assumption that economic analysis can provide us with any "Great Truths" (or even just useful insights) about our economy. Because of the incredible level of complexity and uncertainty in our economy, there are four fundamental problems with trying to use data analysis to develop a better understanding of our economy.

First of all, as we discussed in the previous chapter, because it is impossible for every single price in the world to accurately reflect the TEV of each economic entity, every single price in the world is always "wrong". I shouldn't have to say this, but you cannot perform data analysis on data that is "wrong" and expect to get results that are "True".

Secondly, we need to recognize that when performing data analysis, economists often use various "models" to analyze the data with. These models are generally designed to be a highly simplified version of our economy. Their usefulness is derived from the fact that they are less complex and easier to understand than reality. However, by making these models simpler than reality, we are necessarily introducing errors into the models.

Let us assume that we were able to make an economic model that matches reality perfectly. What we would find is that it had so many variables in it that it would be no easier to understand than reality itself; thus, the model would be of no use to us. The model wouldn't be able to give us any answers that we couldn't get by just observing reality itself.

In order to make our model more useful, we would need to simplify it by replacing some of the variables with what are commonly called "assumptions". These assumptions are generally derived from things that we believe to be true about the world we live in or from things about our world that we wish to ignore due to their complexity.

For example, we could build a model that has a certain interest rate as a variable. If we wish to simplify the model, we could replace the variable of the interest rate, with an assumption about the interest rate. We might decide to hold a certain interest rate steady at 2%.

However, as we saw in the previous chapter, our economy is too large and complex to accurately calculate the price of anything; including interest bearing instruments. So, our assumption about what interest rate we should use in our model will also be wrong.

Thus, the more assumptions you make, the easier the model is to run and understand, but the more errors it contains. The more variables you have, the more closely your model can mirror reality, but the more difficult it becomes to run and understand.

Unfortunately for all of us, economists are not very good at striking an effective balance between variables and assumptions. As I have said repeatedly, people tend to support ideas that fit in with their personal experience with the world. So liberal economists end up making liberal assumptions and conservative economists end up making conservative assumptions.

To make the problem even worse, because our educational system is so horrendous, the vast majority of regular people in this world are not even aware of the trade off made between assumptions and variables. Let alone being capable of distinguishing how the model's assumptions affect its results.

The third problem with trying to use data analysis to guide our behavior also arises due to the failures of our educational system. Because our educational system does a horrendous job at helping people to understand that every single decision in our economy sends us down a completely different path to a completely different economic reality, most people are completely unaware of the fact that our current economy can be thought of as being only one of an infinite number of possible economies.

For example, let us assume that you are in a store trying to decide if you should buy a pair of socks for yourself or a birthday card for your Aunt Gertie. It may seem hard to believe, but your decision is going to send our economy down one of two distinct paths. Your decision will fundamentally alter our economic reality. The problem is that because your decision is so small relative to the massive size of our economy, there is simply no way for us to measure or recognize the impact that your decision will have on the economy.

Because of this, many people have fallen victim to the rather bizarre idea that the economy is somehow being guided by an "invisible hand". *Where do these people think this "hand" is coming from?* I have no earthly idea.

Maybe they think that it is the hand of the boogeyman? Or possibly the fuzzy paw of the Easter Bunny? I don't rightly know. But for some inexplicable reason there are millions of people who seem to ignorantly believe that the market is being guided by some mysterious "hand" floating through the ether of our economy.

In reality, because each decision in our economy is so small, it is impossible for us to see the direct impact that each decision has on the economy. Thus, the economy **appears to move independent of our individual actions**; the market **appears** as if it is being guided by some outside agency or "invisible hand", but the market is not **actually** being guided by an "invisible hand". Instead, the market is being pushed and pulled a tiny, tiny, tiny, tiny amount by every single economic transaction in the world.

In order to better understand the importance of this issue, let us say that we are able to construct a machine that allows us to create separate universes; each of which is small enough for us to observe but still contains an economy that is just as large and complex as ours. The machine further allows us to magically control time in these new universes, so we can choose to have a span of say 50 years pass by in each universe in just a few seconds.

So, we push the start button and immediately a new universe is created, and it runs for 50 years. We push the start button again; another universe is created and it runs for 50 years. Let us assume that we create 50 new universes with our special machine and each universe starts out from the exact same place.

What we would find is that even though each universe started out in the same place, each economy would look different from the others at the end of 50 years (obviously the longer we run the experiment the more variation we would see in the economies). To put this into some perspective, let us consider a similar, but much simpler, exercise.

As everyone knows, if you flip a coin, you have a 50/50 chance of getting heads. So, if you flip the coin enough times, on average 50% of your flips should be heads and 50% tails.

In order to translate this to our economic exercise, let us say that we flip a coin 100 times and we end up with 66 heads and 34 tails. We can call this outcome C1.

We then flip the coin 100 times again. This time we get 57 heads and 43 tails. We can call this outcome C2.

We then flip the coin 100 times again. This time we get 24 heads and 76 tails. We can call this outcome C3.

If we kept repeating this exercise over and over again, what we would find is that some of our outcomes would wind up being very similar to each other, and some of the outcomes would be significantly different. So even though you only have two possible results of each action, and you are only taking 100 actions in each exercise, you can still arrive at very different outcomes.

Now consider that in our economy you have billions of people making trillions of economic decisions every single day over a span of many years and it should be obvious to you that you will naturally see some VERY different outcomes. And it should also be obvious to you that the economists in each of these different universes **are going to come to very different conclusions about the nature of economics** due to the fact that they are all doing analysis on very different sets of data.

That is to say that the economists studying data from universe 1 will come to different conclusions regarding the nature of economics than the economists in universe 2; who will come to different conclusions than the economists in universe 3, etc. In short, it is impossible for the economists in our world to discover any "Great Truths" about economics by doing data analysis **because they are only able to analyze the data from one of an infinite number of possible economic realities**.

The last, and most important, fundamental problem with economic data analysis is based upon the simple fact that it is necessarily constructed upon the results of human behavior. But if that human behavior is being driven by an idiotic belief structure, then the results of that human behavior will obviously not be very meaningful and thus will not reveal any "Great Truths" about the world we live in.

For example, let us suppose that we could travel back in time several hundred years so that we could perform data analysis on our ancestor's behavior. Let us say that we decided to measure how far ships generally sailed from shore to give us a better understanding of the shape of the world.

What we would find is that many ships never ventured very far from shore. *Why*? Because many of our ancestors lacked the navigational knowledge needed for long journeys, they lacked the knowledge of how to effectively store food for long journeys, they lacked the knowledge to accurately predict the weather and some even believed there were giant sea monsters waiting to drag them to the bottom of the sea.

So, our data analysis would not provide us with any "Great Truths" about the nature of the world we live in. Instead, it would have simply revealed the effects of the ignorant belief structure that our ancestors were operating under.

The same is true for our economy today. We could do all the data analysis imaginable, but it still will not reveal any "Great Truths" about economics. Instead, our analysis will simply reveal the effects of the ignorant belief structure that people are currently laboring under; **data analysis will only reveal the effects on human behavior of the myths outlined in this book**.

So, to summarize our situation, here we sit in just one out of an infinite number of possible realities, trying to project the results of data analysis done on incorrect prices, using poorly understood models populated with data that is derived from the actions of behavior driven by an ignorant belief structure onto an infinite number of possible futures. If you needed more proof that human beings are irrational idiots, bon appetit!

Myth 13: Independent Actors

Much of the current debate about what steps need to be taken to improve the global economy is being complicated by the archaic ideology that currently dominates economic thought. Despite the enormous advancements made by science, most economists continue to try and understand the economy using what we might call a "Newtonian" or "mechanistic" view of the world.

Many early economists were so enamored with the clarity and certainty that Newton's Laws of Motion described the physical world we live in, they naturally sought to essentially duplicate his efforts by developing their own Laws of Economics. In their minds, these Laws of Economics would describe and predict exactly how our economy functions with the same clarity that Newton's Laws described the motion of the universe.

Not surprisingly, these economists borrowed many of Newton's assumptions about the nature of reality. So, much as Newton described gravity's mysterious effect on falling apples or orbiting moons, early economists wrote about mysterious market forces and states of equilibrium that inexorably (yet invisibly) pushed and pulled our economy in one direction or another.

And as Newton posited that all observers will see the world in fundamentally the same way, early economists assumed that there is a "Great Truth" in economics that can be agreed upon by all observers; that what is true for one member of our economy is true for all members of our economy.

Where Newton claimed that for every action, there are knowable and discrete reactions (i.e. if I strike the cue ball along a certain line with a certain force, then a certain outcome will always ensue), Economists jumped to the conclusion that for every economic action we take (ex: cutting interest rates, increasing savings, getting an education, etc.), there will be a specific and knowable outcome.

Of course, this mechanistic view of the world is so appealing because it dovetails nicely with our everyday experience with the world. Since we cannot directly see, feel or measure how our individual economic actions affect others, many people have readily accepted the idea that our economy must be guided by something other than our individual actions.

Since the world seems so clear and certain from my own perspective, surely everyone else in the world must be capable of seeing things the same way that I do; surely they can recognize the same "truths" that I do.

The evidence of cause and effect is seemingly everywhere in our world. Thus, it was quite easy for people to assume that it should also apply to economics.

From all of this it is rather easy to see how these beliefs then led people to the assumption that we are all independent actors in the economy. Since the market is guided by outside forces, it is not our individual actions that directly affect the economy. It isn't "my" actions that are making other people poor; it is the "market".

Since I am an independent actor, my economic success is the result of me following the "Great Truths" in economics.

The failings of others are not my fault, it is due to them not following those same truths.

Later in this chapter we will see that when we add in the notion of cause and effect, it is easy for people to reach the conclusion that if people with a college degree get paid more than people who do not, then the college degree must be the "cause" of that effect. Thus, if someone wants to improve their economic standing, they simply need to go out a get a college degree.

The point here being that millions of people have bought into the idea that we are all independent actors in our economy because that idea meshes nicely with our individual experience with the world. Now that we understand why people believe that we are all independent actors, we need to examine the validity of this view of the world.

In order to do this, we need to first take a brief look at the relationship between a Newtonian view of the world and what we might call a "Relativistic" view of the world from the perspective of physics.

In the world of physics, a Newtonian concept of reality can prove to be perfectly adequate when describing the motion of an individual object in our universe. So, if we simply wanted to launch a satellite into orbit around the earth, we could use a Newtonian view of reality to do so. If we measure a specific object from a specific point of view (or reference frame), a mechanistic view of reality works just fine.

However, if we wished to utilize that satellite to provide GPS coordinates here on earth, we would need to use Relativity to account for the relationship between the satellite's movement and the movement of the earth.

Similarly, a Newtonian view of the world can perform adequately when you are only looking at the world from the perspective of an individual or an individual business. For example, if we are only interested in measuring the wealth of an individual named Joe, we can easily see that any increase in his income will be good for Joe, while any increase in his expenses will be bad for Joe.

However, **in order to understand the economy as a whole** (in order to understand the universe of individuals and businesses), we must again begin to borrow ideas from Relativity. We can't just look at the actions of Joe, we need to also account for the actions of others and the effect Joe's actions have on others. We have to consider the fact that if Joe's income goes up, that means somebody else's expenses went up. And if Joe's expenses go down, that means that somebody else's income just went down.

If we try to utilize a Newtonian view of reality when studying the economy, we will always wind up with a paradox or fallacy. We saw in Myth 6 a rather famous example of how such a mechanistic view of the economy naturally leads to a paradox when we looked at the Paradox of Thrift. This paradox is a natural consequence of the misguided belief that saving (i.e. the opposite of spending) is good for the economy.

Adherents to this belief tend to think along the following lines: let us assume that Joe saves 10% of his income. In most peoples' minds, this would make Joe "better off" from a financial perspective. Thus, according to a Newtonian view of economics, if everyone did what Joe did, they would all be "better off" from a financial standpoint. Therefore, the economy would be "better off" if everyone saved more.

However, according to this logic, if everyone saved 100% of their income, they would all be even richer! But clearly this type of thinking is ridiculous because if there was no spending (i.e. there was 100% saving), then there would be no income and the economy would implode.

The reason why a Newtonian or mechanistic view of the economy often ends in a paradox/fallacy is that such a view fails to address the fact that the actions of each economic participant directly **affects all the other participants in our economy**.

In order to understand why we arrived at the paradox above, we have to broaden our reference frame to include ALL the participants in our economy. When we do this, we can see that by reducing his level of spending (i.e. by saving 10% of his income) Joe was lowering the level of income in the economy (as we said in Myth 4: Spending = Income).

Let us say that Joe makes $1,000 a week (we will ignore taxes for this simple example). Let us further assume that in week 1 he does no saving at all. He spends the entire $1,000. This means that Joe will have generated $1,000 in income for the other people in the economy.

Now let us assume that he saves 10% of his income in week 2. So, he only spends $900 ($1,000 * 90%). This means that in week 2, Joe only generated $900 in income for the other people in the economy.

The point being that Joe's saving lowered the income for the other people in the economy. His saving wasn't "good" for the economy. It only appears to be "good" if we only look at the world from the perspective of Joe.

So now we can see that the Paradox of Thrift is simply a result of **trying to transcribe the attributes of a single reference frame to all possible reference frames.** In order to judge the impact to the economy of the actions of any given individual, we need to be able to shift our reference frame. We need to be able to examine those actions from a different perspective.

Because our educational system is so ineffective, there are many people in this world who are simply not capable of changing reference frames. They lack the mental skills needed to move beyond their own personal reference frame. Thus, they can only judge economic ideas based upon what that idea means to themselves; not on what it means to the economy as a whole.

In order to help people move beyond the naïve notion that we are all independent actors, we need to help people recognize the effect that our actions have on others and the effect that the actions of others have on us. The problem is that because the effect on the economy of any one person is so small, we could never see it or measure it in any meaningful way. Thus, we will never be able to go to people and say, *"Here is the specific person that your actions are effecting"*.

Instead, we can only begin to understand the effects of our actions and the actions of others by using logic and reason. As a simple example of this, let us say that you really want to get hired for a job opening as a marketing analyst with Apple. Let us further assume that there are 20 other people who are all applying for the same job.

In order to improve your chances of getting hired, you spend about 1 hour a night brushing up on your knowledge of SQL languages, your data extraction and analysis skills and your knowledge of Apple's products and services.

The other 20 job seekers all go out drinking every night and spend their days laying on the couch surfing through Netflix. Obviously in this scenario you would have a very high probability of getting the job.

Now let us change the scenario. This time around you spend the same 1 hour a night preparing for the interview, while the other 20 job seekers all spend at least 5 hours a night brushing up on their knowledge and skills.

In this case your odds of getting the job would obviously be much lower. Thus, even though you put in the exact same effort, your probability of success was dramatically reduced due to the actions of all the other job seekers.

The point being that the probability of you getting that job is not only affected by your own actions but is also **directly affected by the actions of all the other economic participants**. Whether you succeed or fail in life is not entirely in your control; it will be determined through the relationship of your efforts to the efforts of all the other economic participants.

Thus, not everyone can follow the same path to success in our economy. In fact, if everyone tries to follow the same path, they will so fundamentally alter the conditions of the economy that they will essentially make it impossible for others to find success.

As more and more people attempt to get a job by acquiring a particular skill set, such as coding for example, the increased demand for coding skills will drive up the cost of obtaining it. Even more importantly, as more and more people acquire coding skills, the economic value of that skill set will naturally decline. As we saw in Myth 3, if everybody has some economic entity, that entity will no longer have any trade value; thus, it will have no economic value.

Therefore, if too many people pursue coding skills, the cost of acquiring those skills will eventually outweigh the benefit derived from obtaining the skills. In looking at today's job environment, it is quite likely that we have already reached this crossover point for some skill sets. It is quite likely that there are some people who are already paying much more for a college degree than it is worth.

Many people in this country either have a college educated kid living at home, or at least know of a family that has a college educated kid living at home. One of the main reasons for this is that the cost of a college degree has risen so much that many students leave college with a debt load that prohibits them from being able to afford to start a life out on their own. With more and more people attending college each year, this situation is only going to worsen in the years ahead.

Of course, much of this flies counter to what many economists are preaching about our economy. Many economists ignorantly claim that education is the key to improving the financial well-being of the working class, when we may already be at the point where the pursuit of more education is actually making the working class worse off. By blindly listening to economists who preach about an outdated, mechanistic view of reality, more and more people are being misled into paying more for a college education than it is actually worth.

It may sound strange, but if everyone in this country worked hard and was able to graduate with straight A's from Harvard, we would still have millions of unemployed people and millions of people living in poverty.

If this makes no sense to you, consider what would happen if you went for a job interview in such a world. The interviewer asks "So, why should I hire you?" You proudly stick out your chest and say, "I graduated from Harvard with straight A's!" The interviewer sighs, slowly looks up at you and says, "You see all those people sitting out in the waiting room? They all got straight A's at Harvard too. So why should I hire you instead of one of them?"

Can any one person lift themselves out of poverty? Yes. Because our economy is so large and the actions of one person are so small, there is no limit to what **one person** can achieve. *Does this mean that every individual in our economy has unlimited economic potential?* No. The more people that try to accomplish a certain goal, the more of an impact they have on the economy (i.e. the more they change the initial conditions of the economy).

The point of all this being that, if we ever hope to truly improve our economy, the first thing that must go is the outdated mechanistic view of the economy adhered to by many economists. If this ignorant view of the economy continues to exist, we will continue to be dogged by poor economic decision making.

Myth 14: Self-interest

Another one of the fundamental problems currently facing our economy is the naïve notion that individuals should always act "in their own self-interest". Clearly this idea is derived from the mistaken belief that we are all independent actors in the economy.

As we alluded to in the previous chapter, adherents to a mechanistic view of the economy will generally claim that the people who "succeed" in our economy do so because of their own efforts. On the other hand, the people who "fail" in our economy do so because of their own efforts (or rather, their lack of effort).

From this it is easy to see why so many people believe that each person in the economy should simply act in their own best interest. Since we are all independent actors, if everyone adheres to the "Great Truths" of economics, then everyone will be successful.

Unfortunately, there are two major problems with this ignorant line of thinking. First of all, at the heart of this misguided principle lies the implicit assumption that people are actually **capable** of doing what is in their own self-interest; that people are actually **capable** of doing what is truly best for themselves.

It should go without saying, but for people to be able to make economic decisions that are **truly** in their self-interest, they need to have a very, very sound understanding of economics. They need to be able to recognize both the short-term and long-term repercussions of their decisions.

The sad reality is that because they are so poorly educated, the majority of people in this world **are simply incapable of actually doing what is in their own self-interest**. Because they lack the ability to use logic, most people in this country cannot see the long-term repercussions of their decisions.

People cannot see how chasing the lowest price will invariably wind up hurting their own income. They cannot see how telling corporations to maximize their own value will inevitably lead to reduced investment. They cannot see that excessive levels of saving will naturally lead to excessive levels of debt.

The second, and much more serious, problem with our current concept of self-interest is that it inevitably leads to a very flawed philosophy of life. Because people lack the ability to see the world from multiple perspectives, they tend to assume that "self-interest" means they should not consider how their actions will impact others; that they should only consider how their decisions impact themselves.

Unfortunately for all of us, there are a lot of people in this country whose economic philosophy can be summed up as follows:

> *I really do not care about how my economic decisions impact others. I only care about how my decisions impact me and my family.*

To see why this is such a flawed philosophy, imagine that you run your own little bakery. By telling everyone in the economy to only care about themselves, you are telling them to try and work against your interests as hard as they can.

So, every customer that comes into your store is going to try and squeeze every penny out of you that they can. And every supplier that comes into your store is going to try and squeeze every penny out of you that they can. If you think that it is in your best interest to have everyone in the world working against you as hard as they can, then there truly is no hope for you.

It should be obvious to you that this philosophy is basically the exact opposite of the Golden Rule (i.e. Do unto others as you would have them do unto you). What we are slowly beginning to realize in this country is that by living our lives in complete opposition to the Golden Rule, we are creating a society in which people constantly make decisions that are much too short-sighted. Instead of contemplating the long-term repercussions of their decisions, most people simply focus on *"What does this decision mean for **me** right now?"*

So, for example, instead of recognizing that in the long run any attempt to utilize deficit spending to spur the economy is a fool's game, both political parties have ignorantly pursued that policy **because it makes things better today**. Never mind that any benefits we reap today will necessarily be paid for with pain tomorrow.

People choose to ignorantly pursue lower prices **because it makes them feel richer today**. Never mind that it inevitably leads to lower wages for them down the road.

Because of the seemingly endless stream of selfish, short-sighted decisions being made in our economy, we are reaching a point where it is becoming increasingly difficult for people to trust one another. Businesses don't trust consumers because they know consumers will abandon them at any moment for a lower price somewhere else. Consumers don't trust businesses because they know that businesses will try and cut corners whenever possible to raise their profits. Workers don't trust managers because they know the managers will fire them at a moment's notice just to make their profit targets. Rich people don't trust the poor (and vice versa). Businesses don't trust the government (and vice versa). Businesses don't trust each other; and on and on…

It should be rather obvious, but it is virtually impossible to trust others when you know for a fact that they only care about their own well-being; **when you know for a fact that they do not care about what happens to you**. What we need to understand is that this breakdown of trust represents a major obstacle to getting our economy back on track.

The inability to trust in others breeds a lack of confidence which prevents businesses and individuals alike from "going all in" in terms of investing in the economy. Instead, they hold back and "wait for things to get better", but that holding back only serves to weaken the economy.

The breakdown in trust inevitably leads to a decline in the "animal spirits" needed to ignite the economy. The managers in our corporations are not willing to stick their neck out and fully invest in the economy because they know that any of a dozen other companies will gladly lop the head off those managers to raise their own stock price.

To further complicate matters, with everyone acting only in their own self-interest, it is easy to find examples of "bad people"; "selfish" people whose behavior appears to be ruining our economic system. Thus, pundits from both the left and the right have plenty of targets for their idiotic ideas on economics.

For example, it is currently quite fashionable among conservative pundits to blame the poor for all the damage they are doing to themselves and our economy. Despite the claims of these pundits, however, most of the people at the bottom of our economy are honest, hard-working people. They are simply the unavoidable victims of an economy dominated by the myths outlined in this book.

Does this mean that every single poor person has been trying their hardest to become more productive? Of course not. There are lazy, selfish poor people who try to cheat the system any way that they can (i.e. act only in their own self-interest), just as there are greedy, selfish rich people who try to cheat the system any way that they can (i.e. act only in their own self-interest).

Are there greedy, selfish welfare recipients who are abusing the welfare system in this country? Yes, there are. *Are there greedy, selfish auto mechanics who are overcharging for repairs people don't really need?* Yes, there are. *Are there greedy, selfish doctors who are telling their patients to get unnecessary medical tests performed?* Yes, there are. *Are there greedy, selfish bankers on Wall Street who are milking their customers out of millions of dollars?* Yes, there are.

Despite the claims of economic pundits, however, these people are in the distinct minority. They simply serve as fodder for the pundits to promote their infantile ideas about what is plaguing our economy; from the liberal pundits who blame the greedy, manipulative rich people to the conservative pundits who blame the selfish, lazy poor people.

The fact of the matter is that most people in this country are not "bad" people; **they are just badly educated**. They have unfortunately been trained to believe in the myths outlined in this book; thus, they have simply acted to support these beliefs. The net result is that most people in this country are simply incapable of making effective decisions about what needs to be done in regard to our economy.

It is this ineffective decision making that has led us to the gridlock we see in Washington. The majority of people in this country currently seem to believe that the gridlock is primarily the fault of our elected officials; it is not. It is being driven by the lack of proper economic training in our educational system.

Because most Americans are so poorly educated, they hold very naïve economic beliefs. Not surprisingly, they tend to vote for officials who hold similarly naïve beliefs. Because these officials don't truly understand economics, it is impossible for them to effectively address our economic issues. So, no matter what policies they try and implement, the economy never truly improves and the wealth gap continues to get wider and wider.

The widening wealth gap naturally leads to increasingly different views on the economy between the "haves" and "have-not's. As the economy itself worsens, each side becomes increasingly convinced that it is the fault of the other side. Each side becomes increasingly convinced that the only way to turn the economy around is to implement "their" policies.

Our elected officials are essentially caught in the middle. They are left in the unenviable position of trying to satisfy two extremely different sets of ideas. In general, the Democrats are stuck trying to appease the idiots on the left, while the Republicans are stuck trying to appease the idiots on the right. Neither party is willing to compromise on their policy ideas because neither side can afford to lose their constituency. Thus, we are left with gridlock.

If we continue to follow the myths outlined in this book, the gridlock will end once the working poor outnumber everyone else by such a wide margin that they will be able to elect whoever they want; and implement whatever policies they want. Unfortunately for all of us, their lack of understanding of economics will preclude them from being able to make any effective policy decisions and are thus likely to lead us into yet another financial disaster.

Myth 15: Economics is Vital

In today's world, one will often here people comment that "economics plays a vital role in our existence". This is yet another idea that appears to be true; simply because there are so many people who believe in it. However, just as the idea of the earth being at the center of the universe was not true, eventually people will come to realize that economics plays a much smaller role in our existence than people currently believe.

Somewhat ironically, before there even were any economists, economics used to be much more vital to our existence than it is today. This is because economic activity used to be more focused on providing people with their "needs" (i.e. food, shelter, security, etc.).

In short, our ancestors were much less productive than we are today. Thus, they had a much harder time securing the things that they needed to stay alive. Because their productivity was so low, it took a tremendous amount of people just to produce their basic needs.

Today, because we have become so much more productive than our ancestors, economic activity is now more about satisfying "wants" than it is about satisfying "needs". Because of the reduced dependence on the economy to provide us with our "needs", **economics should be playing a smaller role in our lives**; not a larger one.

By failing to realize this, many people will routinely make political decisions based solely upon whether or not they think that a particular policy is "good" for the economy. There are two problems with this strategy.

First of all, as we have seen throughout this book, many people do not have the slightest clue what is actually "good" for the economy. Secondly, just because something is "good" for the economy does not mean that it is "good" for us as human beings.

To see why I say this, let us imagine that there are two islands: Nofun and Sumfun. The people on Nofun all work very long hours, have no friends, no holidays, no cultural celebrations, etc... The islanders just get up each day, go to work all day and then come home and go to bed.

On Sumfun, the people work about half the day. After work they spend their time with friends and family. In addition, there are many national holidays and cultural celebrations on the island.

Because they work so much (and thus produce much more than the islanders on Sumfun), the islanders on Nofun are considered to be much more successful in economic terms. They can consume much more than the islanders on Sumfun because they produce more.

However, if you ask people which island they would rather live on, most people would undoubtedly choose island Sumfun. So, in our little scenario, it would seem that most people would actually be happier in a smaller economy. I'll bet you never heard an economist tell you that before!

The reason that economists do not tell you this is because they do not believe that such a scenario can exist. *Why?* Because economists ignorantly assume that people are rational, intelligent beings. Thus, economists assume that people will always act in their own "self-interest"; **that people**

will always make decisions that will make them happier (or to use econo-speak, that people will naturally make decisions that maximize their own "utility"). Therefore, economists do not believe that the people on Nofun would work so much if it didn't make them happy.

To the contrary, since people are irrational idiots, **they will routinely make decisions that will make them unhappier**. People will routinely make poor/irrational choices regarding who to date/marry, their diet, who they vote for, their career, about doing drugs, stealing, telling lies, cheating, etc. Sometimes they know these decisions are bad for them, sometimes they do not. But in either case, the decisions often lead to unhappiness.

Within our economy we can see specific examples of poor decision making that ultimately leads to unhappiness. For example, we can see that most Americans generally choose not to learn more about economics (which is a poor decision). Thus, they hold onto ignorant economic beliefs, such as the myth that low prices are good for the economy (which is an irrational belief). Because of their ignorant, irrational belief, they exert as much downward pressure on prices as they can, which inevitably ends up putting downward pressure on their own wages. Thus, they wind up making themselves miserable and they have no idea how or why they are doing it.

The lesson that we will eventually learn from our economic struggles is that to lead a happy, healthy life, we should not focus so much of our attention on economics. Instead we need to maintain a balance of how much time we spend on the 5 main spheres of human existence: economics, health, social interaction, education and spirituality.

Because we currently put so much of our focus on economics, we naturally spend too little time on the other 4 spheres. Thus, we find ourselves failing at each.

It doesn't take a rocket scientist to see how our health (both physical and mental) is failing. We are becoming increasingly obese. Diabetes is rising at an alarming rate. We are becoming increasingly addicted to drugs. Rates of clinical depression have skyrocketed over the past several decades.

Our lack of social interaction with one another is also blatantly obvious. Walk into any venue full of people and you will not find them interacting with one another. Instead, you will find them slavishly staring at their smartphone.

Our educational system is an absolute train wreck. A recent OECD report ranked the US near the bottom among developed countries for literacy, numeracy and problem solving skills.

Our level of spirituality has been declining for decades; with fewer and fewer people regularly attending religious services. Maybe more alarming is the fact that many people who do regularly attend religious services often don't seem to have a clue as to what their religion is trying to teach them.

Because we are failing so badly at all the important areas of our life, there has been a dramatic rise in the level of frustration and disappointment in our lives. You can see it most noticeably in our political process where differing factions routinely scream and yell at each other as if we were on the very brink of total destruction.

All this frustration will only be resolved by improving our educational system. By helping people understand how the economy actually works; and by helping people understand the smaller role that economics should be playing in our lives.

Conclusion: Where do we go from here?

Here is a quick synopsis of our situation. Due to the consumer's naïve obsession with low prices and the misguided directive to have corporations focus exclusively on profits, we have seen tremendous pressure being put on the wages of the working class. This pressure has caused their wages to lag far behind the rate of productivity growth that has been made in the economy.

So almost all the benefits that have come from these productivity improvements have naturally flowed to those people in the economy that were already wealthy. The net effect of this has been a gradual decline in the growth of aggregate demand in the economy over the past several decades.

The downward pressure on wages has also created a rather insecure job market. People are not only frustrated about the lack of growth in their income, but also feel increasingly less confident that they will even have a job in the relatively near future.

This insecurity scares consumers into looking even harder for low prices. The increased demand for low prices forces businesses to cut costs as much as they can, so they hold down wages and scale back investment. This scares workers even more, so they try even harder to find lower prices and the cycle continues.

Because people don't understand the need to invest in productive assets, a disproportionate amount of the profit that we extract from our economy gets diverted into non-productive assets. Therefore, the value of our non-productive assets often rises to unsustainable levels. By the time we recognize this is happening, it is too late, and the stock market comes crashing down (1987, 2000, 2008).

What has made this process so insidious is that it is so gradual nobody even seems to notice that it is happening. Most people know that something is "off", but they can't quite put their finger on exactly what it is. So, they keep doing the same things they have always done, and naturally we keep getting the same results we have always gotten.

In a desperate attempt to increase investment, the government has been implementing a wide variety of measures. Over the past several decades, we have seen tax cuts, massive government spending, extremely loose monetary policy and ambitious attempts to stimulate trade. Despite all these efforts, the economy has continued its inexorable slide into mediocrity.

At this point you should be able to recognize that our government's previous attempts to stimulate growth have all failed because they have all failed to address the fundamental problems facing our economy. Because so many Americans believe in the myths outlined in this book, they naturally elect politicians that support these myths; be they Republican or Democrat. Thus, whatever policies they implement are doomed to fail because they are based upon a flawed understanding of the economy.

The traditional view of economics has always held that if the economy ever hits a recession, demand would fall, which would allow prices to fall. Once prices fell "far enough", the consumer would be tempted to jump back in and start consuming again; thus, restoring demand to the economy and encouraging investors to invest in productive assets. This may be true for an economy full of "consumers", but it is definitely not true for an economy full of "profit maximizers".

For profit maximizers, prices can never fall "far enough" to stimulate demand. No matter how far prices/wages/taxes fall, **the profit maximizer always wants them to fall even further.** Thus, we are essentially caught between a rock and a hard place.

The government cannot do anything to fix the economy because any attempts to artificially inject demand into the economy (through tax cuts or stimulus dollars) will simply create a short burst of activity, but eventually the profit maximizers will grind this demand into profits. Thus, the tax cuts and stimulus dollars will just wind up being even more capital for the bankers to try and find a home for.

At the same time, the economy cannot heal itself because it is being strangled by our naïve belief structure. Our obsession with low prices, saving and high profits will always prevent us from making the investments in productivity needed to fully restore our economy.

So what happens from here?

What we are likely to see going forward is a seemingly endless series of political flip-flops. One political party will gain control and initiate a new set of economic policies; which will inevitably fail to fully turn the economy around. Eventually people will lose faith in that party's ideas, so they will naturally jump ship and decide to try out the other party's polices; which will inevitably fail. And so on.

Throughout all of this, the economy will continue to grow, but it will grow very slowly. In general, real economic growth can come from two main sources: population growth and productivity improvements; both of which are likely to be quite limited going forward.

With the economy stuck in low gear, there is no reason to expect the population growth to pick up anytime soon as people feel too uncertain about their economic prospects to take on the financial responsibilities associated with raising a family.

Not only that, but there are an alarming number of people in this country who actually want to significantly decrease our population! This would have a devastating effect on our economy as it would lead to a serious decline in consumption (which would lead to a serious decline in production).

Similarly, there is no reason to believe that productivity growth will improve anytime soon. There is no reason to believe that corporations will start freely sharing productivity improvements with one another, nor is there any reason to believe that they will invest their mountain of cash into productive assets.

Going forward, any new wealth generated by our economy is naturally going to continue to mainly find its way to the wealthy; just as it is doing today. Therefore, the overall level of aggregate demand in the economy will never truly improve, so the economy will never grow strong enough to justify a significant increase in the level of investment in productive assets. Thus, we are likely to see an ever-increasing amount of capital looking for a home.

With more and more capital sitting on the sidelines, people are going to become increasingly desperate to try and generate returns on that capital. Because they have been burned by the stock market so many times, they are naturally going to be tempted to take huge risks in investments outside of the traditional economy. Thus, the shadow banking system will naturally become an ever-larger part of our economy, putting our entire economic system in an increasingly perilous position.

Even investments made within the traditional economy will become increasingly riskier. With too much capital chasing too little demand, there simply will not be enough safe places to put all that money (particularly if our government makes good on its promise to reduce our federal deficit/debt levels).

In general, our financial position will grow riskier and riskier. All that will be needed to ignite that risk will be a little spark. That spark is likely to come from the working poor in this country.

Societies don't fail during the good times. Societies fail because they are inadequately prepared to deal with the bad times.

With the constant downward pressure on wages, the middle class will continue to slowly deteriorate from the bottom up. The standard of living for millions of Americans will stagnate or, for some, relentlessly decline. Eventually we will reach a point where **there will be so many people at the bottom of our economic system that they will be able to elect whoever they want.**

This large group of disenfranchised people is going to be ripe for a clever, charismatic leader to come along and convince them that they have long suffered from an economic system that has been rigged against them. Of course, this is not entirely true because their own purchasing decisions and their own political decisions have played a large role in their economic demise, but that fact will become increasingly irrelevant. To see why, you just need to think back to our discussion about the fairy who was giving wealth to only half the people on an island.

People's beliefs about the world are not shaped by some "Great Truth" that we can all agree upon; they are shaped by their own personal experience with the world. If too many people grow up in a world where all the wealth constantly winds up in the hands of a few others, they are naturally going to feel that the system of wealth distribution is unfair and needs to be dramatically changed.

To exact their revenge, the working poor will eventually elect a president who makes Barack Obama look like Ronald Reagan. They will demand that we raise the top marginal tax rate to very punitive levels. They will also enact very strict trade policies to protect American jobs from all the "cheaters" on the global stage. In addition, they will most likely place severe restrictions on capital so that it cannot leave this country.

Almost overnight, all the risk that has been building in our non-productive assets will literally explode and **at long last the market will have finally cleared itself of all the excess savings that it has been choking on**.

Wait a minute! How can you say that our economy is doomed when it has clearly been creating millions of jobs over the past decade? Isn't that proof that our economy is improving?

While it is true that millions of jobs have been created since the financial crisis, it is critical for you to recognize the real reasons why so many jobs have been created. There have been three main drivers of growth over the last decade.

The first, and probably biggest, driver of growth has been the excessive amount of deficit spending that has been occurring in our country. Now, normally when you hear the term "deficit spending" it is in reference to the federal government and the fact that it has been borrowing trillions of dollars over the past decade in a desperate attempt to keep our economy growing.

While the federal government may be the largest purveyor of deficits, it is by no means the only entity. In fact, there are several others. In order to recognize this, you simply need to be aware that any entity that spends more than it takes in is essentially running its own "deficit spending" program. So, if you borrow money to buy a car, buy a house or pay for college, you are in fact running a deficit of your own (i.e. you are spending more than you take in). And in case you hadn't noticed, we have had a whole lot of people borrowing a whole lot of money in recent years.

Additionally, many investors have inadvertently been running their own deficit spending programs by pouring trillions of dollars into Silicon Valley and a wide array of IT startups. These investors irrationally believe they have found the next Amazon or Apple, when the reality is that the vast majority of these startups will never be worth a dime.

What they cannot see is that our economy is drowning in capital from all of the excess saving that has been occurring over the past few decades. Thus, it has been surprisingly easy for investors to raise round after round of capital at ever higher prices. Which has helped to fuel a period specific myth such as the ones we mentioned in Myth 11.

At some point the irrational exuberance that currently grips these investors will wear off; leading to a so-called "day of reckoning" (much as it did for the dot.coms). This will lead to a rather dramatic loss of investment value for some investors, which will effectively cut off the excessive funding that is currently bolstering our economy.

So, while all of these deficits do temporarily add demand into the economy and help create jobs, they will not last forever. At some point all of this artificial demand will come to an end, and when it does, real demand will fall, and millions of jobs will be lost.

The second driver of growth in our economy comes in the form of the retirement of the baby boomers. Over the course of the last 30 years or so, the baby boomer generation has been in their prime earning years; thus, they have also been in their prime saving years. From this it shouldn't take a rocket scientist to figure out that some of the issues we have been struggling with in our economy (i.e. excess savings and a lack of investment) have been exacerbated by this massive group of people all trying to save for their retirement.

It is important to note that not only have the boomers themselves been saving, but over the past several decades the government has been saving trillions of dollars to prepare for the impending boomer retirement. In 1980 the total assets in our Social Security trust fund totaled a meager $26 billion. As of 2016 that total had skyrocketed to $2.8 trillion.

Now that the baby boomers are finally retiring, the government is basically mailing out little "stimulus" checks to millions and millions of retired boomers each month. And the number of checks getting mailed out each month will keep increasing for many years to come.

Additionally, the boomers will naturally start spending some of their personal retirement savings. All this spending will obviously add some demand back into our economy and help to eliminate some of the excess capital that we are currently struggling to deal with. Unfortunately, it is not exactly clear how much of a boost that it will provide to the economy or how much it will reduce the amount of excess capital in our system.

First of all, not all of the boomers will spend all of their retirement savings. Many of them are likely to pass on at least some of their retirement funds to their kids. In addition, their retirement spending will be spread out over many years.

More importantly, their spending certainly won't help to change the idiotic belief structure that is currently strangling our economy. Therefore, the benefits associated with this retirement spending are likely to just flow to the top of our economy, thus further widening the wealth gap in this country.

The last driver of growth in our economy is actually closely related to the boomer retirement. No matter where you live in this country, the chances are pretty good that you have seen some new healthcare facilities (hospital, surgery center, urgent care center, doctor's offices, drug store, etc.) popping up in your area. This investment in healthcare is to prepare us for the mounting healthcare needs that will arise due to the aging of America.

Due to the dramatic rise in population brought on by the birth of the baby boomers, combined with a general increase in our life expectancy, we are going to have millions more "old" people in this country over the next several decades. To put this in some perspective, in 1970 there were roughly 20 million people age 65 or older in this country. Today there are about 45 million. And by 2050 it is projected that there will be over 80 million.

This aging of America is fundamentally changing the nature of our economy. It is necessitating large scale investment to prepare us for the onslaught of healthcare that will be needed. This investment is currently creating millions and millions of jobs; from the construction workers who build the facilities, to the doctors/nurses/administrators that work in them, to all the jobs in businesses that provide goods and services to those facilities.

While this is certainly good news for the economy, there are three significant downsides to consider. First of all, this rise in healthcare needs won't last forever. Eventually the number of older people in our economy will level out and thus the need for additional investment in our healthcare system will evaporate.

Additionally, since we have trained business leaders to believe in the idiotic idea that they should maximize the profits of their firm, they have naturally become completely obsessed with controlling costs. Not surprisingly, they do everything they can to avoid training their employees. After all, training costs money; and "costs money" is the exact opposite of maximizing profits.

So instead of having businesses pick up the tab for training our workforce, we have transferred the responsibility for acquiring the appropriate business skills to the working class. There are two fundamental problems with this strategy.

First of all, the people who currently have a job obviously don't see the need to pay for additional training. Secondly, the people who don't have a job obviously don't have the income to be able to afford to pay for the training they need.

So, while we may have plenty of people available to work, many of them lack the skills needed to be productive in our current economic environment. Therefore, businesses are essentially going to be forced to compete for the relatively few workers who have the appropriate skill sets.

This of course is likely to drive up wages (i.e. increase costs) which will likely lead businesses to make much larger investments in IT in an attempt to replace workers entirely.

This is certainly not good news for the people already at the bottom of our economy. They are likely to just get left even further behind which will only add more fuel to their anger; and more political risk to our economy.

The second downside to the increased demand for healthcare becomes obvious when we try to figure out who is going to pay for all this healthcare. Forcing the elderly to pay for their own healthcare may be appealing to many conservative pundits, but from a practical standpoint it is just not very feasible.

Because of the fundamentally flawed design of our current healthcare system, our healthcare becomes more and more expensive every year. So, if we require individuals to pay for their own healthcare as they age, they are obviously going to have to significantly increase the amount of saving they do to prepare for retirement. But this increase in savings is exactly what our economy does not need!

By increasing their saving today to pay for expenses in the future, we will be lowering demand today, which will reduce jobs today and thus make it even harder for people to save for retirement. Alternatively, we could loan out all that savings to keep demand from falling. However, this would only lead to more anxiety about the level of debt in our economy.

Having the government pay for the healthcare of the elderly doesn't appear to be a very viable option either. Many people are already convinced that the government is on the brink of bankruptcy. Thus, proposing that the government pick up the healthcare tab would likely send these people into a frenzy.

In addition, by teaching people the irrational belief that lower prices are good for the economy, they have naturally developed the equally irrational belief that lower taxes are good for the economy. Thus, there are millions of people who will vehemently oppose any tax hike to pay for the healthcare for the elderly.

At this point it is critical for you to recognize that while our economy may be growing and creating jobs, it is not due to our economy being "fixed". The economy is currently being buoyed by the three growth drivers mentioned above. However, the first driver is not sustainable, the second will only last a couple decades and we are unprepared to deal with the needs of the third.

So what should we do?

In order to avoid a disastrous future for our economy, we need to get enough people to recognize the impact that the myths outlined in this book have had on our economy and on our lives in general. The difficulty that we are going to have in trying to do this will come from the simple fact that most people currently don't think they have done anything wrong.

In their minds, the wealthier members of our economy naturally think "I am a good person. I have worked hard and done what I was supposed to do. That is why I have been successful. If everyone else would just work as hard as I do and make the same decisions I have, then everything would be fine."

On the other hand, the poorer members of our economy often think "I am a good person. I have worked hard and done what I was supposed to do. It is the system that is unfair. It is set up to favor the rich. If we just changed some of our tax policies and our corporate regulations, then everything would be fine."

Unfortunately, both groups have completely missed the point. Contrary to what the poor may claim, it isn't our system that is unfair, it is our economic belief structure that is creating the wealth divide in this country. Changing our policies and regulations will do little to change the results we see in our world.

And contrary to what the rich may claim, given our economic belief structure, no matter how hard everyone tries to "get ahead", there are going to be people in our economy who "lose" (just as is the case in the NFL). Even if everybody in the US worked hard and got a college degree, there would still be people stocking shelves at Wal-Mart, there would still be people flipping burgers at McDonalds, there would still be people cleaning bathrooms, etc.

If our ideas about economics are so fundamentally flawed, then why has the American economy grown as much as it has? After all, our economy was almost non-existent roughly 200 years ago; now it is the largest in the world. How could it have grown so much if so many of the ideas that it is built upon are "idiotic"?"

To help us understand why this is the case, consider the following analogy. Let us assume that a man named Dave wants to learn how to play golf. So, he buys a set of clubs and heads straight out to the golf course and just starts flailing away at the ball.

When he starts, he routinely shoots well over 120 strokes per round. But he sticks with it and through a bit of practice and perseverance he develops a little better idea of how to effectively hit golf shots and thus his scores drop down to about 100 shots per round.

At this point, nobody in their right mind would try and claim that Dave knows the "truth" about how to play golf. Despite this, however, he was clearly able to improve as a golfer. The key point to recognize here is that he was able to improve as a golfer, simply by developing ideas about golf that were **better** than the ones he started with. Not by developing ideas that were "true"; just ideas that were **better**.

Now for him to continue to improve, he must continue to develop **even better ideas** about how to properly play the game. He cannot continue to simply hold onto the old ideas that helped him grow as a golfer in the past.

As he improves however, Dave will find that it becomes harder and harder for him to continue to improve. In a sense, he was starting from such a low point (i.e. his ideas about golf were so horribly flawed in the beginning) that it was relatively easy to come up with "better" ideas at first; thus, his game improved relatively quickly. As his ideas about golf improve however, it will become harder and harder for Dave to continue developing **even better** ideas about the game.

The same is basically true of our economy. The American economy began to develop about the same time as the ideas that laid the groundwork for Capitalism were beginning to develop. These early ideas regarding economics were effective, not because they were "true", but because they were **better** than the idiotic ideas that made up the basis of the economic systems that preceded Capitalism (namely Feudalism and Mercantilism).

By adopting these **better** ideas, our economy was able to achieve a level of growth that our ancestors never dreamed possible. However, now that we have achieved all this growth, for our economy to continue growing, it is necessary for us to develop ideas that are **even better** than the ones that have gotten us to where we are today.

To see how this phenomenon plays out in the real world, let us look at the ignorant belief that "low prices are good for the economy". By having consumers so obsessed over low prices, businesses have been forced to try and control costs as much as possible. In doing so, businesses of all sizes have gone to great lengths to make their production and distribution systems much more efficient. This rise in productivity has been extremely beneficial to our economy.

Unfortunately, as we are now finding out, all that downward pressure on prices also creates a tremendous amount of pressure on the wages of the working class. This pressure has led to a marked decline in the economic well-being of the middle class in this country; which in turn has led to a great deal of political instability.

Another example of an idea that has outlived its usefulness can be seen in the naïve belief that corporations should focus exclusively on profitability. While it is true that increasing productivity is one way in which a firm can raise its profitability, it is by no means the only way for a firm to raise its profitability. Other strategies include shipping jobs overseas, holding down wages, busting unions, cutting benefits, moving to lower tax countries, etc.

What we are slowly finding out is that companies much prefer these alternatives to productivity to raise their profits. *Why*? Because they are much easier to implement and provide a more meaningful boost to their profitability.

Businesses in general do not like to invest in productivity because of the inevitable declining returns they would see on such investments. To see what I mean by this, let us revisit our story about Dave learning to play golf.

As we said before, in the beginning, Dave routinely shot well over 120 strokes per round. But by investing a little bit of time, he was able to raise his "productivity" at golf and was able to lower his average score to around 100.

Let us assume that he continues to try and improve his average score. He takes a couple lessons and reads a couple golf magazines. And his average score goes down to around 85.

But Dave is not done yet! He continues to try and improve. He signs up for a series of lessons and reads everything he can get his hands on and spends hours at the practice range. From all of this work his average score drops to around 78 strokes a round.

The key point to recognize here is that by making "investments" in his golf game Dave was able to raise his golf productivity. However, for him to keep raising his productivity he kept having to make bigger and bigger investments; yet he was only able to achieve smaller and smaller increases in productivity.

We see the same thing happen in our economy. Whether someone is learning to build cars, paint houses or write computer code, when they start out their productivity is very low. Therefore, it only takes a relatively small investment to dramatically raise their productivity. But as they become more and more productive, it will take larger and larger investments in time and money for them to continue to increase their productivity; yet they will see smaller and smaller increases in their productivity.

Because our business leaders are trying to maximize their profits, they have no interest in making such investments. They want to try and find small investments with large returns. But because our productivity is already so high here in America, what we need are large investments that will necessarily yield smaller returns. This investment will never happen unless we change the focus of our business leaders.

In addition, it is easy to see that our excessive level of saving that stems from the ignorant belief that "saving is good for the economy" does lead to a seemingly endless supply of low cost capital, which in turn makes investment in our economy more likely. However, it also inevitably leads to mountains of unsustainable debt as our banks frantically try to lend out all our savings.

In all these cases, it should be obvious that we have outgrown the usefulness of our economic beliefs. Those ideas have served their purpose, but now it is time for us to move on and develop the **better ideas** that will be needed for us to continue growing our economy.

At this point many people will undoubtedly jump to the ignorant conclusion that I am one of those folks who believes that we should dump Capitalism for some other form of economic system; such as Communism or Socialism. Nothing could be further from the truth.

The fundamental flaw with economic systems such as Communism or Socialism is that they require a small number of people to make too many decisions that they are simply not capable of making. The world is far too complicated and human beings are far too ignorant for it to be possible to have a group of bureaucrats run our economy. Thus, any form of state-run economy will always fail in the long run because it will not be able to bear the burden of the poor choices the bureaucrats will inevitably make.

By contrast, decisions in Capitalism are not limited to a handful of individuals. Instead, the ability to make meaningful economic decisions is given to literally everyone in the economy. The benefit of this is that the economy becomes much more pliable; the economy can change course much faster and incorporate new information faster.

In a state-run economy you have fewer decision makers, thus each decision they make is very important to the overall health of the economy. Because each decision in a state-run economy is so important, the inevitable mistakes made end up being very costly to the health of the economy.

In a capitalist system, on the other hand, since there are literally millions of decision makers, each decision becomes much less critical to the overall health of the economy. Thus, even though there are many, many poor decisions being made, they do not cause as much damage to the economy.

Even more importantly, **Capitalism's greatest strength is that effectively addresses our greatest weakness.** As I wrote about in my first book *Human Beings are Idiots*, due to the illusion of knowledge created by our thought process, human beings would generally be content to keep doing the same things day after day. To put this in economic terms, farmers would be content to keep raising crops the same way; doctors would be content to keep treating patients the same way; car makers would be content to keep building cars the same way; etc.

Capitalism doesn't allow for this to happen. It forces all economic participants to keep up with those people in the economy that are trying something new; that are looking for a better way of doing things. If you try to hold onto the ideas of the past for too long, you will eventually be run out of business by somebody who has figured out a better way of doing things. Because of this, Capitalism always provides us with an endless stream of new ideas; which is critical for a species as ignorant as ours.

Capitalism's only weakness is that it doesn't do a particularly good job at educating people. Of course, the main problem is that under our current economic belief system an education is only valuable if most people don't have it. Thus, there is essentially no way to increase the amount of education in this country without decreasing the economic value of that education.

In addition, Capitalism is much better at addressing our technical knowledge (i.e. our knowledge of how things are produced) than our general economic beliefs. Thus, we have an economy full of people who are smart enough to be able to design and build smartphones, skyscrapers, electron microscopes, etc.., but at the same time are stupid enough to believe that saving is good for the economy or that lower prices are good for the economy.

Ironically enough, much of the blame for this situation (and for our current economic struggles) can be directly tied to our tremendous level of economic success. After all, if you look at how far America has come in economic terms, it really is quite remarkable. Thus, many people have been fooled into believing that there is no real point in us trying to learn more about economics.

The line of thinking goes like this: obviously we know the "Great Truth" about economics or we wouldn't have come as far as we have. Therefore, there is no need for us to rethink our core beliefs to get the economy growing. Instead, we simply need to change some of our policies or alter the behavior of the "bad" people in the economy (the people who don't follow the "Great Truths").

Since there are so many people who mistakenly view our core economic beliefs as being cherished beliefs that must be defended at all costs, it is going to be extremely difficult for us to make the necessary changes we need to truly strengthen our economy. Instead of addressing the myths outlined in this book, we will undoubtedly continue wasting our time arguing over whether we should raise taxes or cut taxes or reduce spending or increase spending or increase trade or reduce trade, etc. In the end we will still have a nation full of people who ignorantly believe that each individual and each business in our economy should simply focus on maximizing their own value.

I don't think that mankind has yet to develop the words that would adequately express just how idiotic it is for both people and businesses to only focus on how their economic decisions impact themselves. It is the intellectual equivalent of telling all the drivers at a NASCAR race to simply go as fast as they can and not worry about any of the other cars on the track.

The only reason that professional drivers can drive so fast without crashing is that **they are constantly using their judgment as to how fast they should be driving**. They are constantly assessing the track conditions, the weather conditions, the driving habits of the other drivers, the way their own car is handling, etc.

Consumers and business leaders should always be expected to act in a similar manner. They should always be expected to use their best judgment to try and determine how their actions are going to impact others; because that will in turn determine how others are going to act as well.

Instead of just blindly searching for the lowest price, consumers should always consider the character and integrity of the companies they buy from. Consumers should look at the way the companies treat all their stakeholders: customers, employees, owners, the community at large, etc. Sometimes that will mean paying a slightly higher price for an item, but in the long run it will pay off in the form of a better job market and stronger economy.

Business leaders should always look beyond their income statement in order to determine what is in the real best interest of all the company's stakeholders. Instead of naively trying to maximize the value of their individual company, they should always seek to increase the productivity of their company. Sometimes that will mean investing in productive assets even when the economy is not at its strongest, knowing that the increased productivity is what will help to turn the economy around.

The bottom line is this: The Golden Rule wasn't handed to our ancestors on a Hallmark card. They had to learn it the hard way; they learned it by enduring centuries and centuries of pain and misery brought about by selfish, greedy behavior. To think that we can simply throw that hard-earned wisdom out the window and expect this country to succeed is beyond absurd.

Of course, the ultimate irony in all of this is that eventually history will repeat itself once again. What we are eventually going to learn from the economic troubles we have already been through, and from those yet to come if we do not change our beliefs, is that the only way to truly act in your own best-interest is to follow the Golden Rule.

Unfortunately, it is quite likely that many people will simply refuse to believe in all of this. Instead, they will continue to believe that something profoundly intellectual needs to happen. That it will take a sophisticated and intricate set of policies to steer us in exactly the right direction.

Even more importantly, they will continue to believe that it will take something from outside of themselves; that it will require others to change their behavior, but not themselves. That it will require the "guilty" people in our economy to make sacrifices, but not themselves.

The ultimate lesson to be learned from this book is that we are all "guilty". We have all played a role in creating the mess we are in, and it is going to take all of us working together to truly turn our economy around.

www.ingramcontent.com/pod-product-compliance
Lightning Source LLC
Chambersburg PA
CBHW051921170526
45168CB00001B/482